CLOUD NINE: A SEMINAR ON EDUCATIONAL PHILOSOPHY

CLOUD NINE: A SEMINAR ON EDUCATIONAL PHILOSOPHY

by
Norman A. Deeb
Western Kentucky University

PHILOSOPHICAL LIBRARY
New York

Copyright 1975 by Philosophical Library, Inc.,
15 East 40 Street, New York, N. Y. 10016
All rights reserved

Library of Congress Catalog Card No. 75-377
SBN 8022-2165-3

MANUFACTURED IN THE UNITED STATES OF AMERICA

To

All of my students

past, present and future

Foreword

The Esoteric Cult of Philosophy

There are philosophers and philosophers. Immanuel Kant declared that philosophers should speak a universal language, insisting that such was possible—that the mathematician who really understands the most complicated problem can explain it to the man on the street. Then, there are philosophers who take pride in that they communicate only with other philosophers and, sometimes, with only those of their own cult.

There is a tendency for anyone who specializes in any field to develop a jargon, a specialized vocabulary, about his specialty. The mechanic, the athletic coach, the plumber, the doctor, the soldier, the clergyman, the lawyer (obviously)—all have their own vernacular. Sometimes when those of the same craft are together they use common words, because they know they can't fool each other. At a bacteriologist's convention, the bacterium becomes a "bug," for old-shoe simplicity goes better among cronies.

This tendency to develop jargon exists for two reasons:
1) Sometimes there are no ready-made words to fit the new concepts, ideas, and insights which specialists uncover in their work, so they must invent new ones, or "convert" old

ones to new uses—as they do by hooking two or three common words together by hyphens.

2) Specialized jargon "protects," the specialized field from "outsiders," surrounding the field with a charismatic aura that isolates it from commonfolk—the same strategy witch doctors and soothsayers employ by incantations and elaborate trappings.

This is to suggest that, to an extent, specialized jargon evolves out of honest efforts to communicate; to an extent, also, it is a defense mechanism of the specialist who is insecure in his own little field. (Indeed, the tendency for a person to specialize to an extreme may itself represent an escape into something so obscure that there is little likelihood anyone else will explore it and compete with him.)

Now some of philosophy is hard to explain. There are some complex ideas. On the other hand, language provides a ready temptation to increase complexities. The sorting of verbalism that is necessary for clarity from the verbalism that is otherwise motivated is difficult; also, admittedly, the results are inevitably uncertain. Doing so requires both the specialized knowledge and insight of a competent person in the special field and his willingness to accept rejection by his peers in that special field.

From the viewpoint of the special-field jingoist, a colleague who does not join in the incantations and echo the ritualistic terminologies of the cult, who dares to proclaim, as the child did in the Mikado, "There goes the king in his underwear," is a traitor, a heretic, a pariah to be ostracized by the loyal.

Here, Dr. Deeb dares to shout, "There goes the king in his underwear," in this attempt to explain five major philosophic perspectives through a rhetorical device by which he satirizes the cult of philosophy specialists. His own presentations are straightforward, unpretentious, of the clearest, even common, vernacular—in obvious contrast—and again, in satire—to the verbose circumlocutional writings of those who belong to the cult of philosophers today.

The offering here represents a philosophic view that includes such assumptions as these:
1) There is a place for humor in academia—and dullness is not implicit with scholarship.
2) Plain speaking and writing are not out of place in scholarship.
3) It is the responsibility of a teacher to share his scholarship honestly with his students.

The cult of educational philosophers is actually a rather small one—as some within it prefer to keep it! It's not good to mix with "outsiders"; at least one should keep his distance.

It seems unlikely that Dr. Deeb will win many laurels for this work from his peers in the inner circles of educational philosophers. But then—there are others who like to communicate in common-sense terms!

—Paul Street

Professor of Education
University of Kentucky

CONTENTS

Foreword		vii
I	THE PEARLY GATES	1
II	IN LIMBO	15
III	CLOUD NINE	
	SEMINAR ORIENTATION	25
	SUMMARY OF PHILOSOPHICAL TERMS	29
IV	IDEALISM	37
V	REALISM	47
VI	NEO-THOMISM	55
VII	TRADITIONALISM AND AMERICAN EDUCATION	69
VIII	PRAGMATISM	77
IX	EXISTENTIALISM	89
X	THE PROBLEM	101
	A GUIDE FOR WRITING A PHILOSOPHY OF EDUCATION	102
XI	THE EXISTENTIAL MOMENT	113

ACKNOWLEDGEMENTS

It is only proper that I express my sincere appreciation to Western Kentucky University for the sabbatical leave which afforded me the opportunity to write this manuscript. Also, it is not only proper, but it is a privilege for me to acknowledge a number of my colleagues within the university who were very helpful in the preparation of this manuscript:

Dr. Joseph Cangemi, Assistant Professor of Psychology, critiqued the entire manuscript for clarity and continuity.

Dr. Phil Constans, Associate Professor of Educational Foundations and Curriculum, reviewed the manuscript for its philosophical content and objectivity.

Mr. Chuck Crume, Interpretive Naturalist and Wildlife Artist, illustrated the manuscript with appropriate cartoons.

Dr. Carl Kreisler, Professor of Educational Foundations and Curriculum, offered suggestions for the final draft.

Other colleagues who commented on the contents of the manuscript were: Dr. Kenneth Brenner, Assistant Dean, College of Education; Dr. Billy Broach, Coordinator, Educational Foundations and Curriculum; Dr. Emmett Burkeen, Head, Counselor Education; Dr. Gene Farley, Associate Professor of School Administration; Dr. Claude Frady, Coordinator of Graduate Programs, College of Education; Dr. Archie Laman, Professor of Secondary Education; Dr. DeWayne Mitchell, Professor of Counselor Education; Dr. Dorothy Reeves,

Assistant Professor of Secondary Education; Dr. J. T. Sandefur, Dean of College of Education; Dr. John Scarborough, Distinguished Service Professor; and Dr. Robert Sleamaker, Head, Elementary Education.

I am appreciative also to some of my friends at the University of Kentucky for their reaction to the initial draft: Dr. James Moore, Director of Graduate Studies in Elementary Education; Dr. Robert Ogletree, Professor of Educational Administration and Supervision; and two doctoral students, Mr. Carl Banks and Mr. Lynn Moore.

A special indebtedness is owed to the students who were enrolled during the summer of 1974 in Dr. Phil Constans' class and in my own two classes. Those students gave a very frank appraisal of the manuscript and made many suggestions for improving it. Their recommendations did not go unheeded and I am grateful for them.

It would be an injustice to omit Mrs. Bettye Neblett, my typist. Her superior typing was matched by her patience in deciphering my often chaotic scribbling.

I would like to acknowledge my indebtedness to my wife, Rosemary. She not only was very understanding during the writing of this manuscript, but she also guarded, quite cautiously, my solitude. Because of their interest and encouragement, my two teenagers, John and Mark, are also to be acknowledged. They made themselves inconspicuous during the evenings and even added a log or two on the fire, leaving their father free to scribble to his heart's content far into the night.

December 26, 1974

—Norm Deeb

CLOUD NINE: A SEMINAR ON EDUCATIONAL PHILOSOPHY

"Is this Education 577? . . . Er . . . Uh! Flight 577 to Chicago?"

Chapter One

THE PEARLY GATES

"American Airlines Flight 577 is now ready for departure. All passengers may now board at gate number three."

Professor A. Dudley Brainhare picked up his briefcase and proceeded to gate three. The thought suddenly occurred to the professor that flight number 577 was the same number as the graduate course he taught at the university, Education 577, Philosophy of Education. This, indeed, was a coincidence, because the professor was taking flight 577 to Chicago in order to read a philosophy paper at the annual meeting of the National Society of Pedagogical Philosophers.

The professor was very anxious to get air-borne and look over his paper. The semester had been very perplexing as all had not gone well in his education courses. Just the thought of getting away from the campus and sharing philosophical ideas and opinions with other professors was too good to contemplate. His students were somehow becoming more and more boring, because he felt the majority of them were simply not capable of understanding the metaphysical principles involved in developing a true philosophy of education.

The line at gate three was very long, but the professor was totally unperturbed because his mind was completely occupied with his paper and he seemed to have lost temporary touch with reality.

"Sir, may I please see your boarding pass?"

"Er, uh, of course. This is Education 577 to Chicago, isn't it?"

"Flight 577? Yes, sir, flight 577 to Chicago."

"Er, uh, thank you, ma'am," answered the professor as he entered the 707 and made his way to a seat near the wing.

The professor settled back in his seat, fastened his seat belt and the 707 jet soon became a tiny speck in the stratosphere. Finally, the professor opened his brief case and began to read the paper he had prepared for presentation to the National Society of Pedagogical Philosophers:

A Metaphysical Investigation of the Ontological and Epistemological Processes Involved in the Development of a Logic to Support the Theory of Parallelism

Metaphysically speaking, if one were to examine the epistemological processes involved in the investigation of the theory of parallelism, one must begin with Ontology. Ontologically, if one considers any single being, any matter, whether we call it a macrocosm or God, its being will unfold and its reality will be manifested in two forms: (1) The form of a corporeal world (sub attributo extensionis) and (2) In the form of a world of consciousness (sub attributo cogitationis). There is a regular relationship without any specific interaction between the psychical and the physical worlds. A parallelism occurs in both, which implies that whatever occurs in the corporeal world as movement (modus extensionis) appears in the world of mind as ideas (idea modus cogitationis).

Two basic premises are involved in the theory of parallelism: (1) psychical phenomena are not the end products of physical processes; and (2) Physical phenomena are not the end products of psychical processes. Spinoza attempted to substitute an epistemological parallelism for metaphysical parallelism.

Many believe that Spinoza employed the parallelism of the psychical world and arrived at an unsatisfactory solution to the metaphysical question: What is the relationship between thought and being? Spinoza believed . . .

"Excuse me, sir, for interrupting, but may I get you a refreshment or a drink of some sort? Coffee, tea, milk, coke or perhaps a cocktail?"

"Er, uh, arrhumpf. Well, you know it has been a trying day. Please bring me a bourbon and water. No, make it a double bourbon, good Kentucky bourbon if you have it and just a drop of water."

"Anything else, sir?"

"No, young lady, that will be fine."

The professor put his paper aside, made himself comfortable, and began to meditate. The paper was well written, he thought. There was no need to keep reading it. It was very erudite. It would be well received. It contained enough philosophical jargon to impress the society. As long as he would give his own interpretations to the meaning of the philosophical terms, he felt that he would be on solid ground. Then again, he knew from experience that the majority of his colleagues would never question the use of the terminology because it might reflect upon their own intelligence.

"Here you are, sir."

"Thank you, young lady. You are very kind."

The first sip was truly a delight, thought the professor. It was wonderful just to relax and think pleasant thoughts. He had been looking forward to attending this meeting. His paper should be well received. No need to reread it. Very erudite, indeed. For some reason, the professor always liked the sound of "epistemological process" and "metaphysically speaking." The use of such terms always gave him a feeling of confidence. He always felt that his students viewed him as an intellectual giant who could have gone on to bigger positions at more prestigious universities.

"Ah . . . Professor! We have been expecting you . . . !"

The professor sipped his bourbon and his thoughts dwelled at length on how his paper would be received. He concluded that this paper would be the best paper he had ever presented. He suddenly felt very tired and his drink was oh, so relaxing. He could feel the bourbon deep down in his toes.

"Sir, may I get you anything else?"

"Young lady, I'd appreciate a pillow if you don't mind."

"Not at all, sir. Here, let me fluff it for you," said the stewardess, as she arranged the pillow behind the professor's head. He felt so relaxed that, as soon as he nestled his head on the pillow, the professor was sound asleep without so much as his customary thank you.

What seemed to be a short time later, the professor, still very groggy from his nap, found himself in what was apparently a hotel lobby. Although he felt that it was strange to arrive at his destination so suddenly, the professor simply accepted the fact that he sometimes was so preoccupied with his philosophical meditations that it was not unusual for him to proceed occasionally through a part of the day, oblivious to his surroundings. The professor approached what appeared to be the reservation desk, looked at the young man behind the desk and in his best professorial tone announced, "Young man, my name is Dr. A. Dudley Brainhare, and I have room reservations."

"Please come with me, professor. Mr. Peters will wish to talk with you."

"But, young man, all I . . ." Without finishing, the professor looked around and saw a very tall, angular-faced man with dazzling white hair and a beautiful white beard.

"Professor, my name is Peters. We have been expecting you. Would you please step into my private office, as there are certain procedures which we must follow."

"Procedures, what kind of procedures? My reservations were guaranteed by my office and here is my reservation slip for the Conrad Hilton."

"But, professor, this is not the Conrad Hilton."

"Then, what am I doing here? If this isn't the Hilton, then how in the world can you be expecting me?"

"Professor, please try to understand what I am going to say. We have been expecting you since the plane crash."

"Plane crash, what plane crash?"

"Flight 577 crashed into Lake Michigan and all passengers perished."

"Crashed? Perished? You must be kidding!"

"If you don't believe me, come look out this window and look down on earth. You were asleep when it happened. You have left the corporeal world which you referred to as sub attributo extensionis and have entered the world of consciousness of sub attributo cogitationis."

"My God, are you trying to tell me that I'm dead? I can't be dead, I don't feel dead. I'm alive and this must be a very bad joke or a mistake of some sort. Dead? What about my family? No! I don't believe a word of it! How do I get out of here? I have a paper to read! I don't know what big skyscraper I'm on, but I know I'm not dead!"

"Professor, just calm yourself and come over here and look at this screen. This is our internal visualographer, which permits us to do an instant replay as you call it. Here is a replay of you sleeping on the plane. There is the crash and here is a shot of your family in mourning. There is the funeral procession, even the president of the university attended, but you will note that, although there were many faculty members who put in an appearance, there were (tsk, tsk) very few students at your funeral."

"I cannot believe what I am seeing. This must be some sort of a trick."

"Professor, I can assure you that this is no trick. Look out this window. You see those clouds, there are people on them. You are dead and, as soon as you can accept this fact, it will be easier on both of us."

"If I'm really dead, am I in Heaven? Peters? Are you Saint

Peter? Is this the Pearly Gates? Who are you, anyway, and what am I doing here?"

"Professor, you are indeed dead. Incidentally, I prefer the name Pete to Peters."

"But, are you Saint Peters?"

"For the present, please call me Pete. Things have changed drastically since the ecumenical council started on earth. Let's just say you are at a receiving station. Our job here is to screen you."

"What do you mean, screen me? You mean there is a down below, a Hell, and that I might end up there? But I can't go to Hell, what will my students think? Besides, I didn't really misbehave at that convention in Las Vegas. It's true that I didn't tell my wife everything, but I didn't really . . ."

"Professor, for heaven's sake! We aren't getting anywhere with you interrupting me every second. Now you must believe me when I tell you that you are definitely dead and my job is to see that you are processed for an assignment in the psychical world. We have to make sure that your background and qualifications are compatible with the communal assignment you will receive. If you refuse to cooperate, I'm going to note this on your record and send you to, uh, er . . . well, send you to 'that other receiving station'!"

The impact of Pete's remarks was immediately noticeable as the professor momentarily seemed very meek and submissive. Metaphysical questions concerning life and death had always fascinated the professor and he suddenly realized that some of those questions were going to be answered. He also knew that he had better reconcile himself and make the best of the situation.

Assuming what he believed to be his most scholarly countenance, he looked at Pete, gave a gesture of futility and quietly remarked, "All right, Pete, you have my full cooperation. I don't think processing me should be too difficult. However," he added, in a more assured tone of voice, "when

A Hare-Brained Dud
 B.S.—Bull Spreader
 M.S.—More of the Same
 Ph.D.—Piled Higher and Deeper

you assess my qualifications, don't overlook the fact that I have three degrees from three different universities and my students just love me. Surely there will be no problem, no problem at all."

"Professor, kindly permit me to, uh, as you sometimes say on earth, 'tell it like it is.' We can turn on the visualographer and receive instant replays of you teaching chemistry in various high schools. You were voted either the most outstanding teacher or had a yearbook dedicated to you in every high school in which you were employed."

"That is correct, sir. You see, we have no problem."

"But, professor, the situation began to change. You went on to get your Masters, then a Ph.D. in Philosophy. You became a full professor in the College of Education and you had been teaching a course in Philosophy of Education."

"That is correct—precisely so!"

"Professor, let's turn on this visualographer. Here, you are in some high school chemistry classes. I must agree, you did an excellent job. The students really liked you and, better still, they liked and enjoyed the course."

"Exactly, sir! You are a very astute gentleman!"

"Now, let us proceed. After your Masters and Ph.D., you worked in teacher education programs, teaching a materials and methods course related to teaching science in high schools. Your newly acquired background in philosophy made you an excellent choice for teaching a Philosophy of Education course."

"Yes, sir, my credentials are impeccable!"

"Now, professor, let us look at some of your philosophy classes. I want you to really understand how your students perceived you. This shows one of your students sketching a picture of you with the sub title: A Harebrained Dud; B.S. . . M.S. . . Ph.D. . ."

"What! How dare he do that! He called me a harebrained dud! I remember that student. Why, I even gave him an A!"

"Professor, our meeting here is very important. If we didn't

9

think you were capable and consider you worth salvaging, we would not waste our time on you. We would assign you and be done with it. However, you have made things difficult for us since you have become a college professor. The fact that you are teaching philosophy makes our task doubly complicated."

"Why should my teaching philosophy make your task complicated? Every intellectual knows that philosophy professors are considered the most eruditical members in pedagogy."

"Professor, you just said it for me. At one time, at one time, mind you, you were an outstanding teacher. A true credit to the teach—uh, that is, pedagogy, if you prefer. However, your track record since your Ph.D. presents a problem. If you were a bricklayer, an accountant, a chemistry teacher, or if you were in any other field, there would be no problem."

"Pete, I still don't see the problem!"

"Professor, one of your students has identified you with an old, worn-out phrase by saying your Bachelor Degree stood for Bull, your M.S. for More of the Same, and your Ph.D. for Piled Higher and Deeper. Remember the old saying, 'Philosophy does not bake any bread'? What have you contributed to society since you have been teaching a Philosophy of Education course?"

"But . . ."

"Have you solved any problems? Do your students really and truly understand what the basic arguments are concerning educational thought as applied to educational practices? Our visualographer tapes usually show you talking about the 'epistemological processes' involved, or saying 'metaphysically speaking', or constantly using philosophical jargon such as that contained in the paper you were to present to the National Society of Pedagogical Philosophers."

"But, I . . ."

"Professor, don't even speak. Just please listen carefully and try to let this sink in and become a part of your 'reality'. As things stand now, at this very moment we have no place for you. There is nothing you can do for us except play the role of an intellectual or a pseudo-intellectual engaged in the discovery of metaphysical and transcendental properties. Frankly, we don't have time for that. At least, not on this cloud.

"We could send you to Cloud Nine. There you may spend an eternity trying to answer such riddles as how many angels can dance on the head of a pin. You may contemplate the nature of mind, being, existence, or debate to your heart's content the various epistemologies or axiologies which are currently in vogue.

"Professor, we have been patiently waiting for you because you did have, at one time, the ability to communicate with students, though you have neglected to use that ability since you acquired your Ph.D. At one time, you were interested in teaching students how to understand a discipline, and you were an excellent teacher. Since you have been teaching philosophy, you have become more concerned about philosophy as a doctrine. You have become an arrogant, self-centered, egotistical, self-serving individual, who spends his time trying to impress others with his brilliance."

"But, Pete, I . . ."

"No buts. Just listen. You have become a pseudo-intellectual snob!"

"You can't mean . . ."

"I do mean just that, so please compose yourself and listen to my proposition. People like you automatically go to Cloud Nine, where they usually get so sick of trying to impress one another that many end up having nervous breakdowns in the process. We think that you have shown a certain amount of flexibility in your background, as you always seemed to be able to adjust to new situations.

"We would like for someone to devise a Philosophy of Education course which will give students a better understanding of the basic arguments which exist between five philosophical camps—Idealism, Realism, Neo-Thomism, Pragmatism, and Existentialism. We would like for students to know how the basic beliefs have affected education. In your case, because you happen to be from America, what effect has philosophy had on education in America? What effect has educational philosophy had upon educational practice? Many of us believe that it is more important for students to understand why rather than what. To know what happened without understanding why it happened can really have no meaning.

"In short, professor, we want you to humanize your image and teach an experimental group on Cloud Nine. We have isolated a section of Cloud Nine for your use. Twenty-four public school teachers, who are interested in a graduate program, will be assigned to you. These teachers are not only very intelligent, but more important, they also have plenty of common sense. Therefore, I don't believe that you will be able to 'brainwash' any of them. In addition, they represent a cross section of various academic disciplines as well as schools from different socio-economic levels."

"Pete, is there a course syllabus that I am to follow?"

"No, professor, there is no course syllabus, no course outline, no textbook, nor any prescribed materials or methods which you are to employ. We are going to leave you to your own devices. We will terminate the course whenever we wish. You will, however, be given ample time to perform your task which may be more difficult than it sounds. Professor, that's about it. That's all I can tell you unless you have any more questions. We just want you to come up with a practical course in educational philosophy."

"Suppose I decide not to try it. Then what?"

"That, professor, is your prerogative. I could let you see the occupants residing on Cloud Nine merely by turning on the visualographer. Frankly, it would depress you. I know that you are all up in the air, if you will pardon the pun, about being viewed as a great intellectual reading a philosophical paper, but frankly, a view of the occupants on Cloud Nine would be shattering to you at this time. We would prefer that you took another look at yourself teaching in high school. You never felt threatened, you had no image to project—you were simply a good teacher who had some, shall we say, philosophical horse sense. That is why we think you could be our man. We need such a man for this important assignment. Will you do it, professor?"

"You say you will leave me to my own devices. No interference unless you terminate the class?"

"That is correct, but in fairness to you, the only time we will interfere is if we think the situation is absurd or hopeless. You will receive any material or instructional aids you need. The visualographer will be made available to you in the event you wish to review something on earth."

"May I think this over and let you know tomorrow morning?"

"Professor, that will be excellent. Till morning, then."

Chapter Two

IN LIMBO

Almost two months had passed since the professor had consented to teach the philosophy of education course which Pete had outlined. During those two months, the professor had spent many hours trying to organize his course. He had spent a lot of time utilizing the visualographer, which was far more revealing than the professor had imagined. Although Pete had suggested that he specifically review the tapes which portrayed him teaching high school students, the professor also reviewed tapes of his university experiences.

One university tape showed a graduate student bumping into the professor as the professor was leaving his office. The young man muttered very apologetically, "Oh, my gosh, Mister Brainhare, I'm sorry, er, I didn't mean to bump you while I was coming into your office!"

The professor eyed the student very coldly and said, "Young man, I don't know who you are, but my name is Doctor Brainhare or, if you wish, Professor Brainhare! A doctor's degree takes seven years of study and I prefer to be called by my title!" He then gave the student a very disgusted look and added, "Now, what is it that you want?"

The professor was startled when he heard the harshness of his own voice and he could see the student cringe as he mentioned that there should not be any one single yardstick of measurement in any admission policy and the total background of the individual should be considered. The professor could not believe his ears. How could anyone believe such a thing? The majority of today's graduate students, he thought, were incompetent and lazy teachers who were only getting a Masters degree for a pay increment. He believed that any teacher should definitely be denied admission solely on the basis of the GRE scores. The newcomer had no sooner completed his remarks when the professor, in what seemed to be a fit of anger, stood up, waved his finger at the newcomer and snarled, "Then let them go to the Big Ten. Who needs them anyway?" With that, the professor stalked out of the lounge.

The overwhelming majority of tapes showed an unsmiling professor who seemed vitally concerned with his role as a professor and the image he had to project. The professor was really shocked when he viewed some of his philosophy classes. Students never smiled unless the professor's back was turned, and the visualographer had even recorded the derisive whispers which were uttered in his classes. It was evident from the visualographer why he was sketched in cartoons as 'A Harebrained Dud'. The tapes depicted the professor as having the personality of an oyster, the subtlety of a dental drill, and the understanding of Atilla the Hun.

One specific episode showed the professor pacing back and forth in front of the room, waving his right hand in a continuous upward motion and saying, "Metaphysically speaking, when one considers the epistemological processes involved in the analysis of Dewey's ontology of experiences, one has to remember that Dewey believed that there were no ends in education, that the process was the end in itself." The professor paused and, with a very dignified nod, recognized an upraised hand.

"Professor, I'm slightly confused. When you say epistemological processes, are you using processes in the same vein as the process of education, or are you referring to something like epistemological procedures or the logic used in seeking truth? Actually, I hate to admit it, but I don't know how to ask my question because the term process seems to be used in two different ways. Would you please clarify that?"

The professor gave the student any icy stare and then, with a distasteful look, he asked, "Sir, you are an athletic coach, are you not?"

"Yes, sir."

The professor slowly shook his head from side to side, gave a leering smile and, with sarcasm dripping off of each word, he slowly blurted, "Young man, how in the world did you ever get admitted into graduate school and how in the world are we expected to teach when a student even admits that he doesn't know how to ask a question? I suggest that you read Dewey's book, or reread it, if necessary. Then, when you can properly phrase your question, come see me in my office!" If looks could kill, the coach would have died right there.

That was the last episode of university life that the professor would ever rerun. When he saw the stares of disbelief that the students were giving one another, he felt so ashamed that he could not force himself to watch any more. Although studying the university tapes was a traumatic experience for the professor, he massaged his wounds by watching himself hour upon hour teaching his high school students.

It was difficult for the professor to believe that he was looking at the same man. His high school tapes portrayed him as a warm, friendly, outgoing teacher who seemed to really love his work. The tapes were a delight to behold.

One tape recorded young Mark Thomas siding up to the professor and saying, "Mr. Brainhare, I'm in trouble. Can you help me to . . ."

"Why, Mark, I can certainly try," said the professor, with a warm smile. "My, you really look like you are having problems. What's the trouble?"

"Well, Mr. B., I just can't seem to get neuterization to take . . ."

"One thing I want this class to do is to inquire, I mean really inquire. Find something that interests you and inquire about it."

"Hey, wait, wait a minute," the professor chuckled, "Now, Mark, I know you don't mean neuterization, you . . ."

"Oh, gosh, I mean neutralization."

"Well, Mark, do you understand what the word neutralization means? I'm sure you remember that an acid plus a base will give you a salt and water solution. Now, if we test the solution with litmus paper, and it turns red, it is too acid, if it turns . . ."

"Oh, heck, Mr. B. I remember now. My solution has too much acid in it." Mark pointed to his temple, made a circling motion and said, "I must be getting old, Mr. B."

"That's what happens when you reach sixteen, Marko."

Mark smiled, gave the high sign and said, "Thanks, Mr. B." The professor chuckled, patted Mark on the back, and accepted his thanks with a nod and a smile.

Another episode showed Elizabeth Leigh, an eleventh grade student, with an upraised hand. After recognition, she asked, "Mr. B., what effect will the radiation belt around the earth have on our space program?"

"Oh, my! Gosh, Libby, I don't know! I suppose I should know. I can't even tell you I forgot, because I never knew it in the first place. Does anyone know the answer?"

John Geary interrupted with a chuckle, "Why don't you just make Libby look it up, Mr. B., that's what Mr. . . ."

The class began to laugh and the professor interrupted by gently raising his hands and saying, "Now, now, O.K."

He smiled at John and said, "I see no reason for penalizing Libby. Everyone should be encouraged to inquire without fear of punishment. If inquiry ceases because of punishment, then maybe we should re-examine our objectives. Now, Libby," he continued with a very broad grin, "I don't mean to imply that you shouldn't look it up, but I'm not going to hide my ignorance behind a facade and make you look it up." Then, with a more serious expression, the professor surveyed the class and added, "I may not be the smartest man in the world, but one thing I want this class to do is to inquire, I mean really inquire, find something that interests you and inquire about it. Your individual science projects have been great and one of the best things we have done this semester has been our willingness to help one another solve problems." He then raised his fist and, with laughter in his voice, he challenged, "Now, can any of you knuckleheads help Libby and me?"

As the professor reviewed the tape over and over, he was impressed with his own warmth and sincerity. It was evident that there was a great deal of rapport between the teacher and the students. Oh yes, he had his good days and bad days, just like all teachers, but there was no doubt about it, anyone could review those high school tapes and observe a man who genuinely liked students and one who really loved teaching.

For the first time in his life, the professor felt that he had been through a complete process of self-actualization. He could easily understand why Pete had insisted that he utilize the visualographer. The contrast between the high school and university tapes caused the professor to feel a spiritual kinship with Scrooge and the ghost of Christmas past. He had to agree that Pete had been right when he said, "You have become an arrogant, self-centered, egotistical, self-serving individual who spends his time trying to impress others with his brilliance." The tapes had, indeed, been a catharsis.

The die had been cast when the professor, although somewhat reluctant, had agreed to teach the philosophy of education course. He had consented mainly because he felt that he had no other choice except possibly 'that other receiving station'. However, in his soul searching, he realized that he desperately wanted to teach the way he once taught. If he could only walk into a class again and actually establish some rapport with students, he would gladly teach at that 'other receiving station', if they would let him.

The professor had spent a lot of time preparing instructional materials, and topic outlines, which were in keeping with the seminar's objectives. He was confident that he knew enough about philosophy, but how can you possibly teach philosophy without getting inundated with jargon? The university tapes showed the professor so concerned with the jargon, he had never noticed until now that he was unintelligible.

The more the professor thought about it, the more he realized that his big problem was going to be one of communication.

It was very evident in the high school classes that the professor could sense immediately when he was 'coming across' to students, because he had empathy for students. Suddenly the answer seemed so very simple.

Why not teach philosophy of education the way he, himself, had really wanted to be taught when he was in graduate school? Isn't this really the same principle that he used in high school? Somehow, he was going to have to perceive himself in a dual role, both as a teacher and as a student, and establish rapport. He wanted so much to be able to walk into a classroom, let his hair down, and really enjoy his relationship with students. He wanted desperately to be a good teacher again and he believed that he had a chance to succeed. At any rate, he would find out, because the spring seminar on Cloud Nine was to begin the very next day.

"We must be able to disagree . . . without being disagreeable!!"

Chapter Three

CLOUD NINE SEMINAR ORIENTATION

The professor was slightly nervous when he entered the class. He had never felt so ill at ease since his first day as a student teacher. A few of the teachers nodded and smiled and the professor smiled in return. He tried to keep thinking that he was among friends, no need to feel threatened. Everything seemed pleasant enough, but the memory of his university experiences still lingered in his mind. In a sense, he felt like a reformed drunk, but he didn't really know how a reformed drunk was supposed to feel. Self-conscious? Yes, that was it. He felt self-conscious. Wouldn't a reformed drunk be self-conscious his first time out? Well, he must get his mind off himself and think about the students and then, hopefully, everything would be all right.

"Welcome to the first seminar on Philosophy of Education which has ever been held on Cloud Nine. Kindly permit me to introduce myself and explain the purpose of this seminar. My name is A. Dudley Brainhare and I have been asked to meet with this group of classroom teachers which represents a cross section of academic disciplines and schools from many different socio-economic levels in the United States of America.

"Before we begin this seminar, it may be helpful if we had an orientation session and talk about our objectives and how we plan to proceed. In the event you would like to recommend changes in our procedure as we progress, please do.

"First, although there are many different philosophies, we are going to concern ourselves with a cursory examination of only five major philosophies, Idealism, Realism, Neo-Thomism, Pragmatism and Existentialism. As we examine each philosophy, it is hoped that we gain an understanding as to how these philosophies affected educational practice. Philosophy can really be meaningless unless we can understand its effect or implications for mankind.

"Second, to know what happened without understanding the *why* can also have no meaning. Therefore, in our examination of the basic differences, it is very important that we understand why each of the five philosophies subscribes to its particular philosophical position. Once we can understand the why, then perhaps we may become more accepting of the other person's philosophical orientations.

"Third, each of us should be able to formulate his own philosophy of education and have an understanding as to how his philosophy would apply to educational practice. You will be given an outline at a later date and you will be expected to write out your own educational philosophy.

"Fourth, after we have formulated what each of us truly believes to be our own personal philosophy of education, we will spend the remainder of the seminar raising practical questions in education. Each of you will be asked to submit topics for discussion. The topics must be concerned with practical problems in education. These practical problems should be concerned with the process, methods, procedures, or the art of education.

"Fifth, and last but not least, everyone should remember one basic rule. Each of us should be able to disagree with one another without being disagreeable. It is not my intention to try and formulate your opinions and your philosophical beliefs for you. I don't believe that you are that gullible, nor am I that clever. It is hoped that you will critically examine the questions and ideas which will be expressed in this seminar in order that you may crystallize your own thinking.

"Very often, many students are at the mercy of the instructor or text book writer in that students sometimes receive biased interpretations of ideas. Unfortunately this is often true and it would be sheer folly for you to accept my interpretation of various ideas as being the gospel. All you will receive from me will be my personal interpretation of several philosophical views, but it is hoped that my interpretation will be unbiased. I will try to answer any questions which arise by sharing what I believe to be the point of view of the philosophers with whom you take issue. Kindly remember that whatever I say regarding one particular school of thought, there are others who may have different points of view.

"If one wished, one could spend an eternity in philosophical debate and time will not permit us to go into great depth and thoroughly examine five philosophical positions in one seminar. I say this because it is almost impossible to cover completely every facet of every philosophical question. You will merely get my interpretations and this could be misleading, even if my intentions are sincere. Consequently, many of you may wish to pursue some outside reading and I'm sure you will find what you need on the bookshelves which have been stocked for your use. Are there any questions?"

The professor paused momentarily and, in an instant, he quickly realized by the bored expressions that he had been given a captive audience. Pete's voice was still in his mind.

"You must humanize your image and you must not concern yourself with philosophical jargon." In other words, come down to earth and join the group. The professor broke the silence.

"You know, folks, I have a confession to make. For some reason, I have always hated education courses. Science courses, particularly genetics, just seemed to fascinate me—but even heaven refuses to deliver teachers from education courses.

"I suppose that the reason why I detested education courses, particularly in my undergraduate work, was because they were so dry and filled with self-styled opinions which were to be taken as gospel. In order to get a grade in some courses, it was very important to be a nodder. The instructor could say the moon is made of green cheese and, as long as you sat on the front row and nodded, your grade was assured. Now we don't need any nodders in here as everyone reserves the right to disagree without being disagreeable."

The professor immediately noted that more eyes were turned on him and he also noticed a few smiles. Maybe Pete knew what he was talking about. Actually, the professor was really telling the truth as he had perceived it when he was a graduate student.

"In order to understand the philosophical differences of the Idealist, Realist, Neo-Thomist, Pragmatist and Existentialist, we will have to examine their ontological, epistemological and axiological positions and point out how these views have affected educational practices. Oh, I see a hand. Do you have a question, sir?"

"Professor, if this seminar is going to treat philosophy without using philosophical jargon, then I hate to think what it would be like if we used philosophical jargon. Frankly, you have lost me already. I never have had philosophy and I have difficulty even understanding what epistemology and those other terms mean."

"Er, uh, well, now look. Please don't become upset because I have used terms like ontological and epistemological, we shall define the terms we are going to use. Er, uh, you know what? The first philosophy class I ever had really scared me to death. My professor always made statements like, 'metaphysically speaking' and 'epistemological process involved.' If there is anything that I, er, hmm, uh, can't stand, it is someone who must hide his intelligence in philosophical jargon. With some people, not all, mind you, philosophical jargon is a defense mechanism."

The professor began to feel a little uneasy as he wondered whether he was losing the attention of the class. Thank goodness, he had the foresight to have some material duplicated for distribution. The professor quickly distributed a summary of philosophical terms and continued his lecture.

"Now, what we had better do is define what these terms mean. The reason why my first philosophy course was so difficult was because I never understood what was going on until I learned the meaning of various terms. I honestly promise you that, if you will take the time and effort to learn these philosophical terms, you can handle any philosophy course.

Let us turn our attention to this *Summary* of *Philosophical Terms*

SUMMARY OF PHILOSOPHICAL TERMS

PHILOSOPHY—the word comes from the Greek - *Philein*, meaning to love, and *Sophia*, meaning wisdom. Philosophy literally means Love of Wisdom or Love of Knowledge.

I. SPECULATIVE KNOWLEDGE—A division of philosophy which reveals what things are: What is real, what is true, what is good and what is beautiful. Gives man the right kind of convictions which enables him to pursue his final destiny, or ultimate objective. (This view is not shared by all philosophical schools.)

   A. GENERAL METAPHYSICS—Branch of philosophy that seeks to explain abstractions which are beyond the physical or material. Metaphysics may include all aspects of philosophy related to reality, truth, beauty and goodness.

1. ONTOLOGY—A theoretical discipline which is concerned with the study of Reality. It answers one basic question: What is Reality?

2. EPISTEMOLOGY—A theoretical discipline which is concerned with the study of the validity of knowledge. It answers one basic question: What is Truth?

3. AXIOLOGY—A theoretical discipline which is concerned with the study of two values:

   a. Ethics - What is Good?
   b. Aesthetics - What is Beauty?

B. SPECIAL METAPHYSICS—A branch of philosophy which is concerned with special philosophical areas.

1. Philosophy of Man
2. Philosophy of God
3. Philosophy of Education

II. PRACTICAL KNOWLEDGE—A division of philosophy which shows man how he is able to proceed. Practical philosophy is concerned with the activities, procedures, methods or processes involved in attaining primary objectives.

A. How to Build a School

B. How to Organize a Reading Workshop

"First, let's take the word philosophy. Philosophy comes from the Greek—*Philein,* which means to love, and *Sophia,* which means wisdom. The term *philosophy* literally means *Love of Wisdom* or *Love of Knowledge.*

"The early philosophers grouped all knowledge into one large category and referred to various subjects such as astronomy, science, logic, ethics and metaphysics as philosophy. Today we have departmentalized all knowledge into many different categories.

"You will notice that philosophy (Love of Knowledge) is divided up into two main divisions: I—Speculative Knowledge and II—Practical Knowledge. It should be pointed out that it is the Thomists who prefer to make this distinction and this view is not shared by all major philosophies. However, before we attempt to explain the difference, it would be easier if we can gain an understanding of Part A—General Metaphysics.

"*Metaphysics* is a branch of philosophy that seeks to explain abstractions which are beyond the physical or material. In a narrow sense, metaphysics is concerned only with the nature of reality (ontology). In a broader sense, metaphysics includes all of the more abstract disciplines and may refer to speculative philosophy in general. For our purposes during this seminar, metaphysics will include all related philosophical aspects of reality, truth, goodness and beauty.

"Let's look at the terms which are listed under General Metaphysics. All of these terms end in *ology* which indicates that they were originally classified as sciences. However, because these terms are concerned with philosophical abstractions, many philosophers prefer to think of these terms as theoretical disciplines.

"The first term we have listed under General Metaphysics is *Ontology,* which is a discipline which is concerned with the study of reality and it answers one basic question. What is Reality? What does the whole world consist of?

"The second term, *Epistemology,* is a discipline which is

concerned with the study of the validity of knowledge and it answers one basic question. What is Truth?

"The third term, *Axiology*, is a discipline which is concerned with the study of values. There are two axiological categories: The study of *ethics* is concerned with what is good and the study of *aesthetics* is concerned with what is beauty.

"These three terms—ontology, epistemology and axiology—are three philosophical disciplines which are supposed to reveal what is reality, what is truth, what is goodness and what is beauty. As far as this seminar is concerned, whenever you see or hear the word ontology, substitute *reality*, for epistemology substitute *truth*, and for axiology, substitute *values—goodness and beauty*.

"Now to keep from really becoming more confused, let's back up and review. We have thus far identified the three philosophical sciences or disciplines and have explained why they come under general metaphysics. Any questions?"

"Professor, may I ask a question?"

"Yes, sir. Please do."

"Now, if I understand this correctly, ontology refers to reality, epistemology to truth, axiology to values—goodness and beauty, and metaphysics may refer to all of these terms. Then, if these terms are abstractions, would the expression metaphysically speaking make reference to any of these abstractions?"

"Yes, I believe that one could say that, particularly if the term is used in its broadest sense."

"Professor, what is the difference between Speculative Knowledge and Practical Knowledge?"

"Speculative knowledge is concerned with general metaphysical questions which are beyond the physical or material such as what is reality (ontology), what is truth (epistemology), what is goodness and beauty (axiology). Speculative knowledge is also concerned with other special metaphysical areas.

"For example, look at Part B—Special Metaphysics in the

summary (please see page thirty). Philosophy of Man is a special philosophical area which would be concerned with special metaphysical questions such as who is man, where did he come from and where is he supposed to go. Also, the philosophy of man must be concerned with reality, truth, goodness and beauty. *Speculative knowledge is supposed to give man the right kind of convictions which will enable him to pursue his final destiny.*

"*Practical knowledge* guides man as to *how* he is to proceed. *Speculative knowledge* reveals *who, where* or *what,* and *practical knowledge* gives man the practical *know-how.* Speculative knowledge is supposed to reveal to man what his objective should be and practical knowledge lends guidance as to how to reach this objective.

"In education, for example, speculative knowledge would be concerned with the ultimate objectives of education and practical knowledge would be concerned with the practical activities, procedures or processes which involve one man educating another.

"Again, please remember that this view of speculative knowledge and practical knowledge is not shared by every school of philosophical thought. Here is an example which may be used by those philosophers who believe that speculative philosophy has a definite bearing on practical philosophy: If I want to rob a bank, speculative knowledge, according to some schools of thought, would be concerned with one basic question: To rob or not to rob? Speculative knowledge would reveal that bank robbing is a no-no because 'Thou Shalt Not Steal.'

"Practical knowledge would be concerned with one basic question: How to rob a bank. The concern would be the method, procedure, process, or the planning of activities for robbing the bank.

"Maybe it was premature to make this distinction now, because we will need to explore this difference a little later. However, if we can just understand the meanings or definitions of these philosophical terms, I think we will be in

33

good enough shape to proceed without too much difficulty.

"What I would like for this group to do is to study this summary and become familiar with the philosophical jargon. However, for the most part, we are going to try and make this seminar as practical as possible. If we are to achieve the objectives which we have discussed, we may have to stop now and then and take inventory of where we are and how we best ought to proceed.

"Are there any questions or comments on what we have done today? . . . No questions? Well, tomorrow, we will start with Plato's Idealism." The professor surveyed the class, smiled and said, "Till tomorrow, then."

Reality is Mental

Chapter Four

IDEALISM

"Now that we have dispensed with the philosophical jargon, let's turn our attention to the philosophical camps. We said that we were going to examine five philosophical positions and we were going to concern ourselves not only with what was done in education but also with why things were done.

"Today we are going to start with Plato's Idealism and tomorrow we will discuss Aristotle's philosophy of Realism and point out the basic arguments which exist between these two camps.

"Plato was a Greek philosopher who was born over 400 years before Christ, uh, that is, before Christ arrived on earth. Plato is sometimes referred to as the Father of Idealism. In one of Plato's works, *The Republic*, he included his now famous Allegory of the Cave. In Plato's Allegory, he tried to answer one basic philosophical question, What is Reality? We could, if you wish, say this is a metaphysical question or an ontological question. Before we can proceed, however, we must have a common understanding as to what is meant by Reality.

"Reality, as we have used it here, can mean what is real or of what does this entire universe consist. What is this universe that man observes around him? You see, for centuries man had been debating philosophical questions such as: Who is

Man? Where did he come from? Where is he supposed to go? Plato, in order to devise a philosophy which made sense to him, had to come to grips with what is reality. If man could not define reality, it would be difficult to define truth.

"A person could spend an eternity debating the merits, or demerits, if you wish, of Plato's Allegory of the Cave. We are merely going to take a cursory look at his Allegory and talk about its implication regarding truth and education.

"In Plato's Allegory, he pointed out that if we were to take a group of youngsters back into the dark caverns of a cave when they were born, their only concept of reality or what is real would be the dark cave. If we would chain one of the youngsters to a rock and immobilize his head so that he could not see from side to side, but only the dark wall in front, then reality would be limited to the youngster's idea of the dark wall.

"If a bonfire were built behind the person who was chained to a rock, the only concept of reality the individual would have would be determined by the shadows which were reflected on the wall. Plato indicated that if we were to parade humans, animals or perhaps an elephant between the fire and the chained individual's back, the fire would cast a reflection of the elephant on the wall. We could tell the chained man that the shadow was an elephant, but the man's idea or concept of the elephant would be a flat figure on the wall. If we were to unchain the man, he could observe the fire, then he could go to the mouth of the cave and see sunlight. The man may become dazed by the light but all of these things would soon be a part of his reality. If the man saw a real live three dimensional elephant, then his concept of an elephant would have new meaning. Plato believed that man's concept of reality could change, but the change had to take place in the mind because the mind was the center of experience. Therefore, Plato concluded that reality is a world of mind. Whatever this whole universe or galaxy consists of to man is going to stem from his mind, the mind's idea of it."

"Professor."

"Yes, sir."

"Wouldn't reality be a result of the data which we receive through our five senses, instead of concepts or ideas which occur in our minds?"

"Oh, my, how do I proceed after that question? Please don't think I'm hedging. Your question is an excellent one and this problem is raised when one tries to weigh the merits of realism over idealism. In a nutshell, many philosophers, particularly realists, would agree with you, as you shall see later. However, Kant believed that it is difficult for sense data and concepts to be exclusive, one from the other. In order to have concepts, one depends upon the data we gather through the senses. Some realists believe that the mind's existence depends upon sense data. The idealists, however, believe that the mind itself exists independently of sense data."

"Professor, then does this mean that the only thing that is real to man is what his mind tells him?"

"According to the Idealists, yes."

"Well, professor, suppose a person had a nervous breakdown and thought he were Napoleon. Would he then be Napoleon?"

"Well, now, we must remember that the Allegory of the Cave indicated that man's concept of reality could change. If a person believed that he were Napoleon, then as far as he was concerned, he would be Napoleon.

"Let's consider for example a normal, sane, rational individual who suffers a cerebral hemorrhage and becomes paralyzed and is unable to communicate or recognize anyone. The paralyzed person's concept of reality would certainly be a lot different. One could say the person would be living in a different world of reality or living in a different cave. The same thing could be said of the person who thought he was Napoleon. Reality, therefore, would be a concept of the mind and although the concept may depend upon the sense data the mind would receive, the mind, according to the idealists, exists independently of the sense data and is therefore pre-existent."

"Professor."

"Yes, sir."

"It is difficult for me to accept the notion that the mind is pre-existent to sense data."

"Yes, I can understand why this poses a problem for many people. Without getting involved with a lot of metaphysical jargon, let me just point out two things.

"First, Descartes' statement, *Cogito Ergo Sum—I think therefore I am*, is used by many idealists as a reference in making the assertion that it is impossible to know anything without the I, the person, or the mind. Descartes believed that there could be no knowledge without the knower. Many idealists say that if there can be no knowledge without a knower, then the mind is pre-existent to sense data.

"The second point is that the idealists simply believe that there are *two aspects of reality*, both of which are *mental.* One aspect is man's mind, a *microcosmic* mind which is like a tiny grain of sand in the whole universe. The microcosmic mind is the center of man's own little world of reality. The other aspect of reality is the *macrocosmic* mind which is the underlying cause of all the things which exist in the universe. The macrocosmic mind is responsible for casting the shadows on the walls of our cave or for providing all the sense data man perceives. The macrocosmic mind is a world of pure ideas and it is the Absolute Mind. Generally speaking, when an idealist states that the mind is pre-existent he is referring to an Absolute Mind."

"Professor, when you use the term Absolute Mind, are you referring to God?"

"Well, no, not necessarily. There are idealists who believe that idealism has nothing to do with theology. It is difficult, however, to separate the thinking of Berkley, Kant, Descartes and many other idealists from the concept of a belief in God."

"Professor."

"Yes, sir."

"If this course is going to be practical, then frankly it is difficult for me to really understand what we are leading up to. Why should we be so concerned with ontology?"

"That, sir, is a timely question to which we now must address ourselves. We could spend an eternity debating the ontology of mind. That is why I believe that this seminar shouldn't be too concerned about an in-depth study of the idealists' notion of two mental worlds of reality.

"The ontology of idealism is extremely important to the idealist because his whole philosophy stems from his basic premise that reality is mental. If everything in the universe stems from man's mind or an Absolute Mind, then it is a simple matter to define truth. The idealists believe that truth is an idea of the mind, the mind's idea of the sense data it perceives. The Absolute Mind is responsible for producing all the sense data man perceives. The idea of a tree, in fact all trees are ideas of an Absolute Mind. Again, reduced to its simplest terms, if reality were a world of mind, then truth would be either man's idea or an idea of an Absolute Mind. Once man knows what truth is, then it will be a very simple matter to educate man. Let's give youngsters all the truths, ideas, and ideals which they will need."

"Well, professor, who is going to decide what ideas or ideals the child should be given?"

"That is a question which many educators are still debating. The idealist, at one time, believed that education must concern itself with perpetuating certain values. If you remember, we talked about axiology in our summary on terminology (See page 30). We said axiology was a discipline concerned with two values: ethics—what is good, and aesthetics—what is beauty. The idealist believes that man's concept of goodness and beauty would determine the values and ideals which man should seek.

"The idealist believes that goodness is the emulation of the Absolute Mind which inhabits the universe. Good is that which is good for all men. Beauty is the ideal or utopian image. A beautiful painting would not have any imperfections, flaws or ugly features. All works of art should exemplify the ideal and all concepts of goodness should be patterned after the Absolute and should portray goodness for all mankind.

"If we have a basic understanding of the idealist's views on ontology (reality), epistemology (truth) and axiology (goodness and beauty), then we should be able to understand why the idealists believed in the validity of their educational objectives and practices.

"Once the idealist agreed upon what was real, what was true, what was good and what was beautiful, then the formulation of a philosophy of education seemed very simple. The primary purpose of education was to inculcate certain ideas and ideals. If reality were mental, truth were ideas, goodness the emulation of the Absolute Self and beauty the exemplification of the ideal, then the teacher's task was to educate the student by instilling those concepts in his microcosmic mind. In order to become educated, the student needed to know symbols, numbers and the alphabet, to master the art of communication or the arts of expression.

"Once youngsters learned to communicate, it was necesssary to teach them certain truths, preferably those truths, ideas and ideals which have been subjected to the test of time. The curriculum contained many stories with morals and exemplary heroes. Youngsters were given stories which depicted the Spartan life, national heroes to emulate and certain codes of honor to follow. During the educative process, the teacher was expected to be a paragon of virtue."

"Professor, when you say that the teacher was supposed to be a paragon of virtue, what is meant by virtue? Are you referring to chastity?"

"Er, well, no. I can see how the expression 'paragon of virtue' could be misleading. The expression 'paragon' can mean model and 'virtue' can mean excellence. In other words, the teacher would be a model of excellence. The teacher, for example, would never teach youngsters about the harmful effects of tobacco and then smoke outside the classroom. The teacher would never say, 'don't do as I do, but do as I say.' The teacher would set the example by both word and deed."

"But, professor, there are many people who smoke and yet they teach that smoking is harmful. Then, are you saying that these people are wrong?"

"No, I'm not in any position to judge the people to whom you refer. However, at one time, the idealist believed that he should be a model of excellence and he would be wrong if he did not set an example for youngsters. Everything that the idealist did stemmed from his primary goal in education, which was to inculcate or to instill certain desirable ideas and ideals into youngsters, to teach them to think, to make them aware of all the great writers, artists, thinkers and philosophers.

"We must also remember that, in Plato's time, we had the slaves, some peasants, some literate merchants, warriors, the upper ruling class and the intellectual statesmen. Education, per se, was for the elite. The most important subject on earth at that time was philosophy. Science had not yet achieved the distinction of really being a true discipline.

"Colleges which originated in early America usually were started as theological colleges and the curriculum was primarily concerned with philosophy, theology and the classics. As the philosophy of idealism evolved over the centuries, much emphasis was placed on the study of classical subjects, such as literature, the arts, philosophy, languages, history and mathematics. Some colleges introduced a curriculum whereby a student would study one hundred books which comprised some of the works of our greatest thinkers. Practically every liberal arts college in the United States can look back to the idealists for the philosophical justification for their very existence.

"Sometimes, the liberal arts are referred to as the 'elitest education'. At any rate, to this very day, some professors in the liberal arts sincerely believe that knowledge for the sake of knowledge or for the fun of knowing is the most important aspect of education. However, it would be wrong for me to imply that liberal arts professors feel that a college of science and technology is undesirable. Nevertheless, a true idealist, for reasons only known to another idealist, would place himself on a higher rung of the educational ladder.

"Idealism had a tremendous impact on education. The liberal arts completely dominated the whole spectrum of American higher education until the twentieth century. This dominance had an effect on elementary and secondary education, but we will discuss that later. Our purpose in this brief treatment of idealism was, hopefully, to gain an understanding of the underlying reasons for the positions of the idealist and its effect upon educational practice.

"You are not expected to accept or to reject the philosophy of idealism at this time. Although you will be expected to consider its merits or demerits as they apply to your philosophical beliefs, it will be to your advangage, I believe, to hold any final judgment until we have covered all five philosophies. Later, some of you may find that you may not feel completely comfortable in any one camp, although many do.

"Are there any questions about what we have done today? Well, if there are no questions, please remember that, as soon as we finish looking at the other philosophies, we are going to have group discussions concerning philosophical thought and practical classroom problems. Let's adjourn until tomorrow."

Reality is Things

Chapter Five

REALISM

"At our last meeting we talked about Plato's ontology of mind and the philosophy of idealism. The idealist believed that reality was mental and truth was an idea. The purpose of education was to teach youngsters ideas which reflected the ideal and perpetuated deeds for the common good of society. During the process of educating the 'microcosmic mind' of the learner, the teacher was expected to be a paragon of virtue, one who taught by word and deed. The curriculum consisted of certain truths, ideas, ideals and values which youngsters were encouraged to attain. Exemplary heroes were always a part of the curriculum. Knowledge for the sake of knowledge led to the establishment of liberal arts colleges.

"Now, before we continue with realism, our next philosophical camp, are there any questions concerning idealism? . . . Well, then, let's continue.

"There were a number of philosophers such as Anselam, Machiavelli, Spencer, Russell and many others who helped to develop the philosophy of realism. Although the contemporary philosophy of realism may have a somewhat different meaning, Aristotle can indeed be referred to as the Father of Realism.

"Plato established a school outside of Athens and Aristotle enrolled in Plato's Academy when he was 17 years old. He that it was Aristotle's ontology of matter which aroused his interest in nature and science. Aristotle was the first philosopher to elevate science to an exalted position in the order of knowledge.

"One of his major contributions was in the classification of knowledge into various branches such as physics, metaphysics, logic, poetics and psychology. He laid the foundation for many sciences. Aristotle believed that through *induction* one may examine particular principles and arrive at general principles in science. He also attained great distinction by formulating a method of logic called *deduction* or *syllogism* and he was considered to be the greatest authority on logical reasoning for many centuries.

"Yes, ma'am, you have a question?"

"Professor, could you please use some examples and explain the difference between the inductive method of reasoning and the deductive method of reasoning?"

"I believe so. First, let's take Aristotle's logic of syllogism or deduction. The basis of this logic is that we must begin with a general truth and seek to connect it with an individual case by means of a middle term or class of objects which are known to be equally connected. Then we deduce the *specific* from the *general*, attributing to the specific the distinctive qualities of the general. For example:

> All men are mortal
> Kilroy is a man
> Therefore, Kilroy is mortal.

"What we have done is that we started with a general truth (All men are mortal) and connected it with an individual case by means of a middle term (Kilroy is a man), then *deduced* a new truth (Kilroy is mortal). What we have done was to go from the general to the specific.

"Now, *induction* is a method of reasoning whereby we examine a sufficient number of individual facts and on the basis of analogy state that what is true of them is also true of others of the same class, thus *arriving at a general principle*. For example, if we were to take a group of acids and neutralize each of them with a selected number of bases, we would, in each case, end up with a solution of salt and water. After we have arrived at the same conclusion in each individual case, we then can arrive at a general principle or law which states that an acid plus a base will yield a salt and water.

"It should be emphasized that the early philosophers attached great significance to Aristotle's syllogistic deduction, more so than contemporary philosophers. Although Aristotle gave much prominence to deduction, he constantly raised an important question concerning how do we know the validity of the major premise from which one begins his deduction.

"Although Aristotle's ideas have generated disagreement for many centuries, realists generally agree that matter or things exist outside the mind, independent of any knowledge of its existence. Man can observe, examine, and test things or principles and arrive at scientific conclusions which are based upon fact. Many realists believe scientific conclusions, or facts, are more reliable than philosophical or metaphysical conclusions. Many realists also believe that the most important truth is fact, that which can be verified by empirical evidence.

"The realists believe that if nature is responsible for all the many wonders of the universe, then man should become aware of his surroundings and explore all the mysteries of nature. Consequently, axiology should be concerned primarily with nature; goodness should be man's conformity to the natural order; and beauty should convey a natural image. The realists believe that if reality were a world of matter, truth were fact, goodness subject to the laws of nature and beauty the duplication of nature, then our educational objectives should be quite obvious. Educators needed to bring all these things into the classroom. Let the teacher demonstrate all the wonders in nature by conducting demonstrations in science, giving youngsters all the facts and information they need, and then the youngsters would respond to the stimuli or to the facts and information received from the teacher.

"Although methods of instruction may have changed, realists at one time believed that the teacher was a demonstrator, one who would demonstrate facts or principles of science as opposed to one who was a model to be followed. The student, rather than being a microcosmic mind, was believed to be some sort of sense mechanism which responded to certain stimuli by means of the senses. A major purpose of education was to give each youngster all the facts and information he would need for the world outside of the classroom. In order to accomplish this, a great deal of emphasis was placed upon drill and rote memorization.

"The realists can share the responsibility for the great advances of science and technology. In higher education, especially, all colleges of science and technology are rooted in the philosophy of realism.

"Yes, sir, you have a question?"

"Professor, this breach as you called it. Does this mean that the idealist does not believe in science and the realist does not believe in philosophy?"

"Oh, no! Not at all. I should have been very emphatic in explaining that it would be erroneous to believe that either philosophy would totally reject the other. It is just that each philosophical school would give primary importance to its own philosophical beliefs. Now it would be ridiculous to assume that the idealists do not believe or could not accept any scientific principles. They do, but they believe also that philosophical principles are more important than scientific principles. To the idealist, the College of Liberal Arts is more exalted than science and technology.

"The idealist has his world of ideas—the classics, the humanities and knowledge for the love of knowledge. The realist has his world of things—things which may be verified by empirical means. Many believe that the contemporary realist is preoccupied with science and the idealist is preoccupied with philosophy. Although we are at an impasse, it would be erroneous to assume that either denies the existence or the importance of the other.

"If there are no further questions, tomorrow we will take a look at the Thomist. Many believe that there may be similarities in that Thomism may be a combination of both idealism and realism which is centered around God.

"Nevertheless, till tomorrow, and we shall see."

Reality is Being and God

Chapter Six

Neo-Thomism

"In order for us to have a better understanding of how Neo-Thomism differs from idealism and realism, it may be worthwhile to briefly review a few important points.

"Plato's Allegory of the Cave was the basis for the idealists' ontology of mind. They believed that the mind was responsible for interpreting the shadows on the wall of our cave and knowledge could not exist without a knower. Consequently, reality was considered to be a world of mind and truth was an idea of the mind. The primary purpose of education was to instill the microcosmic mind of the learner with ideas and ideals from all the great writers, artists, thinkers and philosophers. The teacher was expected to be an exemplary model, one who taught by word and deed. Eventually, the idealists' quest for knowledge for the sake of knowledge led to the establishment and growth of liberal arts colleges.

"The realists believed that things, such as that flower we referred to in Gray's Elegy, could exist outside the mind, independent of man's thought of it. Reality was believed to be a world of matter or things—all of the things which are abundant in nature. Man could observe, examine and test things or scientific principles and arrive at scientific conclusions which were more demonstrable than philosophical conclusions. So, instead of philosophy, the realists thought that educators needed to emphasize scientific demonstrations in the classroom. They reasoned that youngsters were sense mechanisms which responded to certain stimuli or facts. Accordingly, a great deal of emphasis was placed upon rote memorization. Although the methods of instruction may have changed, the realists are primarily responsible for the establishment and rapid expansion of colleges of science and technology.

"It is obvious that we have not made an in-depth study of either idealism or realism, but it is hoped that you understand why the idealist emphasized ideas and ideals and the realist emphasized facts and information in the educative process.

"Are there any questions or comments concerning either idealism or realism? O.K. Let's continue with Neo-Thomism which I prefer to call just plain Thomism.

"In the 13th century, or over 1600 years after Plato and Aristotle initiated their philosophies, Thomas Aquinas, an Italian theologian, could not and would not accept the notion that God did not play a vital role in reality. Aquinas believed that man was a creature composed of body and soul which was inseparable until death.

"Aquinas was intrigued with Aristotle's matter-form hypothesis which he studied and elaborated upon. Aquinas differed with Aristotle in that he believed that the *Principle of Actuality* provided *Existence* instead of form, and the *Principle of Potentiality* provided the *Essence* instead of matter."

"Well, professor, what difference does it really make?"

"Very frankly, to the overwhelming majority of people, it really doesn't make any difference at all. However, to any philosophical scholar who was attempting to pursue this logic in order to arrive at a rationalization for including God in the educational curriculum, it would seem important. The principles of Potentiality and Actuality are related to *teleology* which is a theory that man or the entire universe is moving towards a final union with God.

"Very simply, the Thomists believe that Pure Essence and Pure Existence is God, the First Cause or the Prime Mover of the universe, who determines the ultimate destiny of man. According to the Thomist, man's movement toward his final destiny is determined by the ultimate objectives of education which are to know, love and serve God. Once man has learned certain pre-determined truths and values, then man will know how he ought to proceed in order to achieve his final destiny.

"Aquinas formulated an ontology in which he stated that reality was a world of *Being*. He believed that there were two kinds of beings: (1) logical beings—ideas or concepts which exist inside the mind; and (2) real beings—real things which exist outside the mind.

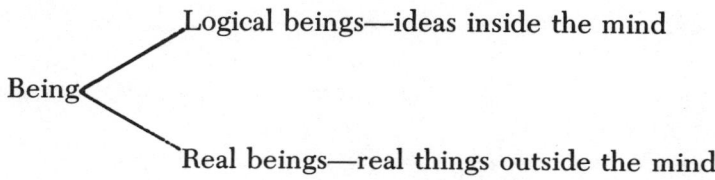

"Aquinas believed that ideas could exist inside the mind and that things could exist outside the mind independent of man's thought of them. He also believed that ideas could exist inside the mind which may achieve existence and ideas could exist inside the mind which could never achieve existence."

"Professor, isn't it possible for any idea to achieve existence?"

"Well, to some philosophers, it may be debatable. The Thomists believe that ideas may exist inside the mind which may achieve existence; for example, finding a cure for cancer. They also believe that ideas may exist inside the mind which could never achieve existence. For example, the idea of a square circle may exist inside the mind, but by its very

57

definition a square circle could never achieve existence outside the mind. We may say that nothing exists in a vacuum or two minus two equals zero or nothing. The meaning of the term nothing exists inside the mind, but nothing does not exist outside the mind. The Thomists believe that ideas may exist inside the mind and things may exist outside the mind. They also believe that the mind may intuit eternal truths which will be true throughout eternity."

"Professor, what do you mean by eternal truths? Are you referring to God?"

"Well, yes and no. The Thomists believe in two kinds of eternal truths: one, Absolute Truth with capital *A* and capital *T*, which is a divine truth and which refers to God; the other, *a*bsolute *t*ruth with a small *a* and small *t*, which is not a divine truth because it is not directly related to God. Aquinas believed that eternal truths are revealed to man's mind through man's intuition. He also believed that man may reason facts. The facts which man acquires through reason would not be eternal truths because man can err, or because new facts may be discovered later which can cause man to change his findings. Truths learned through reason were referred to as practical truths. They may be true for all time, but they also may be subject to change.

"Let me pause here and see if there are any questions or comments."

"Professor, it seems to me that Aquinas' ontology of Being is really nothing more than the combination of Plato's world of mind and Aristotle's world of things joined together and called Being. Also it seems that when Aquinas says that truth is reason and intuition he is really combining Aristotle's truth is fact and Plato's truth is an idea. Is this a valid assumption?"

"Your assumption is an interpretation which is shared by some philosophers."

"Well, professor, what I don't understand is how or why does the Thomist believe that man can intuit an eternal truth, a truth that may or may not be divine. Can you give an example?"

"Well, let me first just generalize in an attempt to explain the Thomist's position as simply as possible. Unfortunately, there is really no simple explanation, but let's try.

"First, let's take faith. We have truths based on faith, human faith and divine faith. By accepting human faith, we accept truths on another person's word or authority; by a divine faith, we accept truths on God's word or authority which we refer to as *Absolute Truths*. Now *Absolute Truths* are supposedly revealed to man through man's intuition. For example, the story of Moses and the Ten Commandments.

"When Moses was on Mount Sinai, the Ten Commandments, as the story goes, were literally written with the fiery finger of God upon the stone tablets. The Ten Commandments were revealed to man. They were self-evident; the commandments revealed themselves. According to the Thomist, man did not think up or reason out the Commandments because they were a divine revelation. Man did have to reason out the meaning of the Commandments but his mind was not responsible for their existence."

"Well, professor, suppose, I mean just suppose, that someone on earth did not believe in God, then what?"

"You know we could attempt to pursue Aquinas' logic and discuss matter, form, essence and existence of Pure Being. However, our purposes in this seminar are not that esoteric. Regardless of the amount of rhetoric one uses, as some theologian once said, for those who believe in God, no proof is necessary; for those who do not believe in God, no proof is possible. Saint Anselam of Centerbury had a motto which was taken from Saint Augustine: *Credo ut intelligam*—believe and you will understand. In other words, any creditable logic which explains God must depend upon Faith.

"I think I know what may be troubling you so let me attempt to explain this another way. The Thomists believe that all knowledge stems from sense perception and this perception includes the mind as well as the sense data the mind receives. The mind, according to the Thomist, depends upon the senses in two different ways. The way the mind depends upon the senses will determine whether the truth which is revealed to the mind is eternal, will never change, or is a practical truth which may be subject to change. Let's look at these two methods of dependence.

"The first method: The mind depends on the senses both for the understanding and the enunciation. This method of dependence may be referred to as *necessary dependence.* Necessary dependence means that it is necessary for the mind to use the senses for understanding a proposition as well as enunciate it. Our mind depends upon the senses to *reason* out new truths and to enunciate truth. For example:

"Let us say that we have conducted some experiments and we have been using the inductive method of reasoning and have enunciated a proposition such as all matter is composed of atoms. It was necessary to use the mind's thinking process to arrive at this truth. We can then, by deduction, arrive at other truths by saying that a tree is matter because a tree occupies space and has weight; therefore, a tree is composed of atoms.

> All matter is composed of Atoms
> A tree is Matter
> Therefore, a tree is composed of Atoms

"Now, we started with a proposition, all matter is composed of atoms, and we were able to proceed to new truths. According to the Thomist, it was necessary for the mind to use the senses for arriving at the truth and also to speak or enunciate the proposition. Therefore, because the mind used reason when arriving at the truth of the proposition, the expression, 'all matter is composed of atoms', is true today and may be true for all time, but it may be subject to change. Why? Because man used reason. Man is capable of error when the mind is used as a measuring instrument. Man is fallible. Whenever the mind depends upon the senses both for the understanding and the enunciation, we have a practical truth which may be subject to change."

"Well, professor, what seems to be controversial about that? Isn't this generally accepted by most concepts of epistemology, that man may err and truth may change?"

"Yes, this is acceptable to most schools of philosophy, but the argument begins when the Thomist says that there is another method whereby man attains truth.

"The second method: The method mind depends on the senses only for the enunciation and not for the understanding of the proposition. It is only by accident that the mind learns new truth without using a reasoning process. The mind just tends to know.

"The mind *intuits* truth. The mind depends upon the senses only for saying or enunciating the truth. This method is referred to as *accidental dependence*."

"Oh, I think I see now, professor. You mean God. Man knows by intuition that God exists. We have absolute truths which are believed to be attained through intuition."

"Well, we have said that we were not going to try and point out how logic is used to verify the existence of God, an *A*bsolute *T*ruth, but it is important that we understand how the Thomist arrives at the notion that there are *a*bsolute *t*ruths which are eternal and unrelated to God.

"We said that the Thomist believes that all knowledge stems from sense perception and this includes the mind. The mind depends upon the senses in two ways. The first way was called *necessary dependence*; the mind depends on the *senses both for the understanding and the enunciation*. The second way is called *accidental dependence*; the mind depends on the senses not for the understanding, but *only for the enunciation*."

"Professor, how can a person enunciate a truth without understanding what he is saying?"

"Well, it's not that a person would not understand the truth, it's just that it is believed that he did not have to reason the truth out before he knew it. The truth revealed itself to him. The truth was self-evident. If man uses reason and arrives at truth, we say the truth is evident. Now, self-evident as used by the Thomist means that the truth revealed itself to man and man knows through his intuition. Let's look at an example of small *a* and *t*, absolute truth, which is used by the Thomist:

$$\text{The } \overparen{\text{Whole}} \text{ is Composed of its } \overparen{\text{Parts}}$$

"Once man arrives at a definition of the word *whole* and the word *parts*, it becomes self-evident to man that the *whole is composed of its parts*. The subject element whole and the predicate element parts are integrally related. Man learns this through his intuition. The proposition revealed itself to man. Man did not have to reason the truth because it was self-evident.

"The Thomist really tries to reduce the argument down to one basic factor in regard to truth. How did man learn it? If he used necessary dependence and reason, the truth, although evident, may be true for all time, but it may be subject to change. If man arrived at truth by means of accidental dependence, man's intuition told him the truth was self-evident; the truth then would be an eternal truth and never subject to change."

"Professor, there is a point that seems to confuse me. You stated, I believe, in the proposition that

$$\text{The } \overparen{\text{Whole}} \text{ is Composed of its } \overparen{\text{Parts}}$$

that the subject element, whole, and the predicate element, parts, are integrally related. Well, what about

$$\text{All } \overparen{\text{Matter}} \text{ is composed of } \overparen{\text{Atoms}}$$

Aren't the subject element, matter, and the predicate element, atoms, integrally related? Why couldn't this line of thought make the proposition 'all matter is composed of atoms' an eternal truth?"

"That is a good question, but let's back up and review. Remember, we said that, in order to arrive at the proposition, all matter is composed of atoms, it was necessary for man to depend upon his senses to reason out the proposition. Grammatically speaking, the subject element matter, and the predicate element atoms, are connected. However, they were not integrally related by definition. Man had to reason out the proposition and proceed to new truths. Truth learned through reason may be subject to change.

"In the proposition, the whole is composed of its parts, the subject element, whole, and the predicate element, parts, are integrally related by definition. Hence, the argument goes that man attained this truth through his intuition and it will therefore be an eternal truth or an *a*bsolute *t*ruth with a small *a* and small *t* because the truth is unrelated to God."

"Well, then, professor, of what importance would this be to a seminar of philosophy of education? Actually, what difference does it make anyway?"

"Well, to many people, it probably doesn't make any difference at all. The reason why we have been concerning ourselves with Thomistic epistemology is because of the impact that Thomism had upon education in America.

"First, I should point out that the concept of an *a*bsolute *t*ruth, small *a* and small *t*, is important to the majority of theologians, regardless of their church affiliation. Remember that Aquinas developed his Philosophy before the Protestant Reformation. Most theologians agree that their particular church has as its major function to spread the word of God. In order to do this, there must be a rationale for God's existence. Since some people say that man cannot prove that God exists and man cannot prove that He doesn't, they may conclude that man just doesn't really know.

"Theologians are very concerned with the logic of God's existence. Most or many churches believe that, if acceptable logic can be used to validate the existence of an absolute truth that is not divine, then the logic which is used to validate the existence of an Absolute or Divine Truth may be less difficult to accept. Now our purpose here is to point out that the Thomist believes in eternal truths and we should have an understanding of the impact Thomism had upon education.

"The Thomist believes that there are two main divisions of philosophy. If you will remember our summary on philosophical terms (see page 29), the two main areas of philosophy were called speculative philosophy and practical philosophy. Speculative philosophy, according to the Thomist, is that branch of philosophy which consists of general metaphysics—ontology (reality), epistemology (truth) and axiology (goodness and beauty). Speculative philosophy is supposed to tell man what is real, what is true, what is good and what is beautiful. Speculative philosophy is supposed to tell man what things are. Speculative philosophy is supposed to tell man, who is man, where did he come from, and where is he supposed to go. Speculative philosophy is supposed to determine the ultimate objectives of man. Speculative philosophy, according to the Thomist, is supposed to give man the ultimate objectives of education. Therefore, Speculative Philosophy is supposed to give man the right kind of convictions which will aid him in solving his practical problems and pursuing his final destiny.

"Practical philosophy is supposed to tell man how to proceed or determine the process, the activities, the procedure or the method of education. *Speculative philosophy* would be concerned with educational questions such as what is the *ultimate purpose of education. Practical philosophy* would be concerned with *how man can best educate other men.*"

"Professor, I still don't follow that line of reasoning because it is difficult to understand how speculative philosophy has any bearing on helping man solve his practical problems. For example, a number of years ago, I operated a gas station in California. When the gasoline shortage occurred, I couldn't meet my payments because there wasn't enough gas to sell. Believe me, professor, that was really a problem. Now, how would speculative philosophy have a bearing on my solving that problem?"

"Well, actually, in your case it probably wouldn't have had a bearing, but it could have, according to the Thomist. Man solves many problems without even thinking of speculative philosophy. Suppose, let us say, you decided to rob a bank in order to meet the payments on your gas station. Meeting the payments would be a practical problem, but how you secured the money could be related to a speculative problem. As we mentioned in our orientation session, *To Rob or Not to Rob*, that is a speculative question and, according to the Thomists, a no-no because 'Thou Shalt Not Steal'. How to meet the payments or how to rob a bank would be a practical question concerned with practical philosophy. The Thomist believes that speculative philosophy may have a bearing on helping man solve his practical problems. The Thomist does not mean all practical problems.

"The Thomists were primarily concerned with saving the 'soul' as well as educating the individual. They believed that the teacher was the spiritual leader in the classroom and should be primarily concerned with disciplining the mind of the students. Goodness was believed to be inherent in the object and certain things ought to be desired because they are good. A good act was a reasonable action resulting from rational thought. Beauty was that which was pleasing to the intellect. Values were usually related to morality and a great deal of emphasis was placed upon moral and spiritual values.

"Although the teacher was vitally concerned with the training of the intellect, a great deal of emphasis was placed upon knowing, loving and serving God. The Thomists believed that attaining God is the ultimate objective for man and that schools should aid man in developing intellectual tastes, habits, knowledge, skills, ideals and values which will enable man to effectively serve his God, his family and all mankind.

"Are there any questions concerning Thomism? O.K. It seems that we may have spent a lot of time on these first three philosophies. But, if this is going to make any sense at all, then at our next meeting, we should start examining the effect of these philosophies on American education.

"Are there any comments or questions about what we have done?"

"Professor, what about the outline and the philosophy paper we are to write?"

"Oh, yes, we will have to talk about your paper, but don't worry about it now. We'll talk about your paper after we finish pragmatism and existentialism. Any further questions or comments? O.K. Folks, I'll see you tomorrow."

"I pledge allegiance to the flag of . . . . . one nation, under God with . . . ."

Chapter Seven

TRADITIONALISM AND AMERICAN EDUCATION

"It was mentioned during our first meeting that philosophy may be meaningless unless we can understand its effect or implications for mankind. It is also meaningless to know what happened in American schools unless we understand the *why* or the philosophical justification for the total educational program.

"In our first few meetings, I tried to present a short analysis of the metaphysical questions which the traditional philosophers examined in their attempt to validate their educational objectives. I believe that we should now pause and briefly discuss the effects of idealism, realism and Thomism on education in America.

"The idealists maintained that the teacher should be an exemplary model for youngsters to follow. Ideas and ideals which have stood the test of time should be included in the curriculum. Knowledge should be learned for the sake of knowledge and schools should aid in perpetuating the national heritage.

"The realists, although sympathetic with the educational objectives of the idealists, were primarily concerned with all of the things which abounded in nature. They thought that the teacher should demonstrate scientific principles and that youngsters should be taught all the facts and given all the information they would need outside the classroom.

"The Thomist's main concern was to give God a place in the educational process. They theorized that man is a creature composed of body and soul which are inseparable until death. Therefore, their concept of educating the whole child was to develop the intellect and to teach Absolute Truths so that man may know, love and serve God in order to achieve his ultimate destiny.

"There is an educational theory, I might add, which believes in the philosophical positions of both the idealists and realists. The *essentialists*, who espouse the theory of *essentialism*, believe that in order for any youngster to be educated, there is an *essential body of knowledge* which must be transmitted. This body of knowledge would come from both the idealists and the realists. Youngsters should be given symbols, ideas, exemplary models, knowledge of their cultural heritage, facts, information, knowledge of the world around them and the ability to use both the inductive and deductive methods of reasoning. In other words, the *essentialists* believe that basic ideas, ideals, facts and skills which are essential to our culture should be taught to all youngsters by time-tested methods.

"There is another educational theory which shares the position of the Thomist. Because eternal truths are supposed to be true year after year after year, they have been called *perennial truths*. The *perennialists* are those who believe in *perennialism*, the theory that there are truths that are eternal. Therefore, moral and spiritual values would be included in the curriculum. Incidentally, it should be pointed out that a perennialist is not necessarily a Thomist because there are other schools of philosophy which believe in perennialism.

"It is quite possible that there are those who may disagree, but it seems that public education in early America was really influenced by all three of these philosophical schools — idealism, realism and Thomism. Although there is no philosophical school called Traditionalism, I prefer to think of all three of these schools as being a traditional concept."

"Professor, when you say that Thomism influenced education in America, do you mean the Catholic Church?"

"No, ma'am. I am not referring to the Catholic Church, as such, but Thomistic philosophy. Again, we must remember that Aquinas initiated Thomism in the 13th century before the Protestant Reformation. Religious groups may differ in practical philosophy such as the liturgy of the mass, communion, individual activities or social restraints, but they generally agree that speculative philosophy has a value in helping man to solve his practical problems. This is the basis for including the teaching of moral and spiritual values in the curriculum. The overwhelming majority of religious denominations believe that man's concept of what is true, what is good, and what is beautiful gives man the right kind of convictions to pursue his final destiny. The Thomists were primarily responsible for formulating a philosophical basis for including God and moral and spiritual values in the schoolroom.

"Now, whether one would agree or disagree with any particular philosophical camp is really a moot issue. The idealists, realists and Thomists each made a unique contribution to public education in America. An American philosophy emerged which seemed to embrace all three of these philosophical schools of thought which we will refer to as traditionalism.

"There are many people who get a little perturbed about the purpose of education in early America. Today, we may hear educational objectives which make reference to society and the right of the individual. However, before we condemn the pilgrims for being so short-sighted and for not writing educational objectives which were all encompassing, let's examine the social circumstances at that time.

"Actually, what was there to know? Man had not yet invented the telephone, the automobile, television, the computer, jet travel, nor visited the moon and started other space adventures. Man was still in the ox-cart age. The Christian

Ethic of 'keeping your nose to the grindstone and your shoulder to the wheel' and observing good moral Christian practices was the key for man attaining his just reward, both on earth and in Heaven.

"Let me briefly mention a few historical landmarks or events which reflect the influence of traditionalism on American education.

"When the pilgrims landed in New England in early 1600, all of the men helped one another to build homes for their families. The next thing they built was a Church and a school. Their educational objectives were clearly spelled out and they did not need a graduate course to think through their philosophy or purpose of education. The primary purpose of education in early America was *Education for Salvation of Souls*.

"In the New England colonies, the child's first training was in a Dame School, which was conducted by a neighbor. The school was held from several weeks to a year. The teacher conducted school and did her housework at the same time. Reading, writing and fundamental doctrines of religion were the primary subjects. The first core curriculum in the Puritan School was the *Catechism*.

"The Reading and Writing School was the forerunner of today's elementary school. The New England Primer was utilized for teaching reading and writing. The book contained the alphabet, syllables and phonetic structure of words. Reading, writing, spelling and ciphering were learned in 2 or 3 years. The school was taught by the minister and much emphasis was placed upon the Catechism. The minister was expected to set an example by word and by deed. He was the spiritual leader as well as the mental disciplinarian. Memorization and strict obedience were the methods of instruction.

"The Latin Grammar School took the boy from the Reading and Writing School and prepared him for college. The Latin Grammar School, which was later replaced by the Academy, was the forerunner of the high school. A great deal of emphasis was placed upon the classics and a fluent knowledge of Latin and Greek was necessary for admission to college. The first college in America was Harvard which was founded in 1636 for the purpose of training ministers.

"In 1642, Massachusetts passed a compulsory education law to see that all youngsters would attend school, learn to read and write and understand the principles of religion and the capital laws of the country. No method was provided, however, for doing this.

"In 1647, the Deluder Satan Law was passed which required towns to support schools. A tax was levied on the number of children a family had in school and poor children were admitted free. The purpose of the law was to see that every child attended school in order that he learn to read the Bible. Once a youngseter could read and understand the Bible, then he could delude or escape Satan and save his soul.

"In the Middle Colonies, the Dutch settled at New Amsterdam, the Quakers in Pennsylvania and the Catholics in Maryland. Each religious group, like the Puritans, wanted instruction in their own particular faith. The greatest contribution of the Middle Colonies was the Academy, which was the forerunner of the modern high school.

"The wealthy plantation owners in the South had private tutors for their youngsters and, after they reached their teens, many were sent up East to 'finishing schools'. There were pauper schools established for those unable to afford tutors. A system of apprenticeship was established whereby a young lad would be given a home and taught to read and write. He was able to learn a trade, but the most emphasis was placed on service.

"One may readily recognize that these historical events reflect the influence of traditionalism on American education. Most early educators gave first priority to education for salvation of souls and this priority remained in many schools for over 200 years.

"In 1793, after the Revolutionary War, America moved from Colonial status to Independence. In 1787, Congress provided that 1/16 section of each township was set aside for schools. New England had set a pattern for compulsory education and taxation. The practice, however, took almost a century to spread.

"The establishment of schools was left to individual states. Civilization began to spread westward. America needed maps, deeds, surveyors, bookkeepers and more educated citizens. Schoolmarms slowly began to replace the ministers. A system of education was beginning to grow. Because the social conditions began to change, new demands were made upon the educational system. The educational objective, salvation of souls, was clearly not adequate to meet the needs of America.

"The new nation needed to establish a feeling of pride in its citizens. U.S. History was introduced and much emphasis was placed upon the young nation's heritage. A new philosophical objective emerged to supercede 'education for salvation of souls' and it became *Education for Citizenship*.

"In the 19th Century, McGuffey's Reader began to replace the gloomy New England Primer. Rote memorization remained as the primary method of instruction. Spelling bees became very popular and Noah Webster's Spelling Book was utilized in practically all schools. Good spelling and proper grammar was a mark of gentility.

"In 1844, Horace Mann was the first Secretary of the State Board of Education in Massachusetts. Mann's annual reports influenced American education. He outlined the need for school buildings, better libraries and better teachers with adequate training for each classroom. He advocated the inclusion of music, art, science, English, math, history, literature, hygiene, physiology and physical education in high schools. One of Mann's primary objectives was the establishment of a free, universal and non-sectarian school system under state guidance.

"In 1872, the first high school to be built from levied taxes was built in Kalamazoo. The citizens took issue with the purpose of the tax and fought the action in court. The court sanctioned the building of the new school. Compulsory education and taxation meant keeping records. Teachers needed more training as the curriculum which Mann had advocated in 1844 was slowly being introduced. Very few youngsters attended high schools, which, in reality, were college prep schools. Because of the need for bookkeepers, bookkeeping became an elementary subject. Manual training, geography, nature study and music also were introduced into the curriculum.

"Teachers began to attend institutes for three or four weeks of training. Then came Normal Schools to train teachers which later were expanded into teachers colleges. An example was the establishment of Teachers College, Columbia University in 1898.

"The age of the schoolmarm was at its zenith with the one-room schools, McGuffey's Reader and the spelling bee. Education in America was for the most part traditional. Although the educational objective was primarily *education for citizenship*, the impact of the essentialists and the perennialists could not be denied.

"Traditionalism served public education well. A primary objective was placed upon education for citizenship with a great deal of emphasis upon moral and spiritual values. As America grew, its needs grew also. This placed a great demand upon the public schools. To help America meet its needs, the pragmatists arrived on the scene with a prescription which many considered to be a pill too bitter to swallow. Nevertheless, the social circumstances seemed to be ripe for the battle that was to follow. When the dust finally settled, the pragmatists had initiated some of the most controversial educational changes America had ever known.

"If there are no questions, we will adjourn for the day and, tomorrow, we will discuss pragmatism and its impact on American education."

Reality is Experiencing

Chapter Eight

PRAGMATISM

"Before we begin pragmatism, let us reflect for a moment and see where we are so that we will have a better understanding of the philosophical breach which developed between the traditionalists and the pragmatists.

"Thus far, we have discussed the basic philosophical differences between the idealists, realists and Thomists and related how each philosophy affected education. We put all three philosophies in one group, called them traditionalism and briefly touched on how traditionalism affected American education.

"We must bear in mind that the traditional concept of education is primarily concerned with essentialism and perennialism. Traditional schools, whether public or private, may use modern educational methods of instruction. In fact, many of them do. However, a traditional public school, in the philosophical sense of the term, will be unyielding in its insistence on the importance of two major aspects of education. First, they believe that there is an essential body of knowledge which should be imparted to all youngsters. Second, they believe that speculative philsophy has a bearing on practical philosophy. Therefore, they believe that moral and spiritual values should, and can, be included in the instructional program without teaching religion.

"Before we make any hasty judgment, we should consider the social circumstances which prevailed in early America when the purpose of education was *education for salvation of souls*. Later on, after the Revolutionary War, the purpose was changed to *education for citizenship*. The most important thing to understand, however, is that whenever a culture undergoes change, it cannot always be assumed that the educational objectives of one generation can be transferred to later generations and remain valid. One of the biggest tasks in education is to help students meet the challenges which they will face in a rapidly changing society.

"The 20th century found America a young and vital nation which was to experience the greatest industrial growth of any country in the history of the world. Public education could not keep pace with the industrialization and urbanization of America. Schools began to consolidate and school districts began to merge. A number of educators began to influence educational systems which were growing all over America.

"Pragmatism was a philosophical movement which was founded by John Dewey, Charles S. Peirce, William James and George H. Mead. Although Peirce, James and Mead made very significant contributions, Dewey left an indelible mark upon almost every public school in America. Pragmatism is also known at times as 'instrumentalism' and 'experimentalism'.

"Dewey did not believe that it was absolutely necessary to go to speculative philosophy and use 'metaphysical principals' to arrive at an ontology. Although the world consisted of things and man was endowed with a mind, he felt that it was the interaction of the thing, the objective conditions, with the internal conditions of the mind. Dewey referred to this interaction as a situation which provided man experiences. Dewey maintained that individuals lived in a world of situations and their concept of situations and interaction was inseparable. Therefore, Dewey concluded that *reality was a world of man's experience.*

"Dewey could never accept the notion that man's destiny was determined by forces surrounding him or that man must live under the guidance of unchanging truths. Dewey was convinced that ideas should be weighed against the consequences of experience rather than accepting a truth as being self-evident. He believed that if man had a problem which habit or impulse could not solve, he should develop a plan of action or an hypothesis which would best solve the problem with supporting evidence.

"From 1894 to 1904, Dewey headed the department of philosophy, psychology and education at the University of Chicago. In 1896, he set up an experimental elementary laboratory school in order to test methods whereby children could *learn by doing.* Dewey viewed education as a process of living rather than a preparation for later living.

"The children in the laboratory school were given the freedom to have experiences in line with their interests while the faculty studied their behavior. Dewey was able to test and develop many of his ideas on philosophy and psychology. He was instrumental in advocating the application of the scientific method to moral and social questions."

"Professor, how can you apply the scientific method to moral and social questions?"

"Hmm, well, that question probably signifies the biggest gap between the traditionalist and the pragmatist. Please let me back up a little in an attempt to give you a better understanding of the argument.

"In one of Dewey's books, *Democracy and Education,* he wrote about the purpose of education, social consciousness, the nature of the individual and the process of education. Actually, he focused on two main points.

"First, Dewey said there were no ultimate aims in education; educational objectives are never final. The only end in education is the *process* itself. Dewey stated very early in his book that education is a constant process of reorganization and reconstruction of immediate experience.

"What Dewey meant was that society was rapidly undergoing change and it was the duty of the school to provide the kinds of educational experiences that would enable a youngster to function in a changing world. Because the world was changing, the educational objectives and the process of education must constantly be evaluated and modified to meet the demands of society.

"Dewey wrote a great deal about the democratic process and democracy in the classroom. He believed that youngsters should enjoy a certain amount of freedom to explore various areas of interests. He did not view education as being subject centered, whereby certain subjects were systematically drilled into every child. He preferred to think of education as being child centered and that teachers taught children rather than math, English or science.

"Rather than utilizing the demonstration method in science, Dewey advocated science laboratories whereby students could *learn by doing*. He strongly insisted that if education were to be meaningful to youngsters, then youngsters should have the opportunity to learn from their own experiences. Science laboratories, art, pottery, crafts, industrial arts, home economics, school plays, debating teams and other extra curricular activities are a few examples of educational experiences which could be very meaningful to youngsters.

"Dewey introduced what he called the project method of instruction. For example, if a science teacher were getting ready to introduce a unit in science on The Sea Around Us, he would let the class decide what phase of the sea they would prefer to study as a project. Several committees could be formed and each committee might undertake a project to study and make a report to the class on such a subject as crustaceans of the sea, the effect of the moon upon the tides, mammals of the sea, whaling, the shrimp industry or any other topic which a particular student or group of students would like to undertake. The teacher was not a mental disciplinarian, a model or a spiritual leader. He was a democratic coordinator who aided youngsters and gave direction and support to class projects. Dewey was convinced that the unit would be more meaningful if students were allowed the freedom to make choices. The teacher was expected to utilize the democratic process in arriving at a decision which affected the class. Dewey felt that if youngsters were going to function adequately in a democracy, they must experience the democratic process in the classroom."

"Well, professor, what happens when the students utilize the democratic process and vote to do something the teacher thinks they shouldn't do? Then what?"

"That, indeed, did cause a problem, one which caused Dewey's critics to raise a loud cry of protest. Unfortunately, some of Dewey's followers misunderstood him as they literally permitted youngsters to do as they pleased. Of course, this did cause chaos in some classes.

"In a later book, *Experience and Education*, Dewey said that an experience may be enjoyable, yet at the same time cause a youngster to be careless, unresponsible or indifferent to learning. Dewey explained that some experiences may be mis-educative as well as educational. In other words, some experiences are good and some experiences are bad and it is the duty of the teacher to provide the right kind of experiences.

"Well, Dewey's critics charged that he had finally admitted that if the teacher were obligated to provide the right kind of experiences to help shape attitudes, then he had to agree that speculative philosophy and the ultimate aims of education were necessary in order for his philosophical position to have validity.

"Dewey rebutted that the values and attitudes which youngsters had formulated during the educative process should reflect the values and attitudes of a democratic society. Society, and not speculative philosophy, should, as far as

Dewey was concerned, reflect or determine what values should be imparted to youngsters.

"Dewey later changed his definition of education from 'education is a constant process and reorganization and reconstruction of experience' to 'education is a constant process and reorganization of *socially desirable* experiences.'

"Dewey concluded that society should decide whether a value was good or bad and that we should judge things in light of the consequences of the experience. What effect did this experience have upon the individual or society? The pragmatists believed that things were neither good nor bad in themselves apart from their effects. Let's put it to the test of experience and see what happens and judge the experience in the light of whether it works. If it doesn't work, let's modify it and try again.

"The traditionalists argued that if you start out with probable knowledge in a hypothesis you will end up with probable knowledge. Science cannot define values because values are in the realm of the metaphysical. Science can only judge things in light of whether it works.

"I think probably that it should be pointed out that the cultural mores of America were just beginning to experience a drastic change. Women's suffrage, divorce, smoking, dancing, birth control, card playing, tithing and many other moral questions were being raised. The traditionalists were fearful that Dewey's philosophy could undermine man's concept of 'speculative values' because the notion as to whether things were good or bad could not, as far as the traditionalist was concerned, hinge upon whether it was socially acceptable. The traditionalists were ready to fight to the death on one major point, social acceptability.

"Social acceptability was not sufficient condition for accepting the desirability of a value. An example, let's say, is that in some cultures it is socially acceptable to steal. Just because it is socially acceptable, the traditionalists believe that this is not a sufficient condition to say that it is good to steal and let's teach youngsters how to steal.

"Ironically, the argument was a philosophical argument. One could always utilize examples on each end of the continuum and evoke the response that this isn't what was meant. However, the traditionalist was primarily concerned that speculative philosophy should give man the right kind of convictions which would enable him to pursue his final destiny. Practical philosophy would be concerned with a process of education which would enable a youngster to serve his God, his country and also become a good citizen in his community.

"The pragmatists believed that speculative philosophy had no bearing on education and the only end in education was the process. The process must constantly be reorganized and reconstructed to meet the needs of a changing society. Dewey believed that traditional schools were giving youngsters the wrong kinds of educational experiences. He felt that traditional education consisted of subject matter which had been worked out in the past, along with certain rules of conduct and moral and spiritual values, and the primary task of the school as viewed by the traditionalist was to transmit them to every generation of youngsters. Books were the instruments for transmitting the knowledge and teachers were the disciplinarians to see that the knowledge and moral values were transmitted. Dewey charged that traditionalism is autocratic and that the process of traditional education was beyond the scope of youngsters' experiences because that which is taught is a finished product and has little regard for the changes which may occur in the future.

"When Dewey said that some experiences are mis-educative and it was the teacher's duty to provide the right kind of experiences, he was talking about instructional experiences. He felt that traditionalism had caused many students to lose the incentive to explore ideas because of the way learning was experienced by them. Dewey felt that automatic drill may have enabled individuals to acquire special skills but the individuals' ability to make decisions in new situations was limited.

"Dewey maintained that his views on educational progress were more compatible with democratic ideology because the instructional methods were more humane than the harsher autocratic policies of the traditional school. Schools were social institutions run by the will of the members of society. Social acceptability, therefore, had to be a very primary consideration when planning the curriculum or all the experiences in which a child could participate at school. Dewey's philosophy gave rise to what was later referred to as the *progressive* movement in education.

"It seems that the progressive movement started an awakening or an awareness of the contributions which could be made by the people in the community or by society in general. Curriculum planners began to consider the needs and wishes of the local citizenry. Social studies became a requirement of study in all schools because it was believed that, in order for man to adapt to society, he should understand the society in which he will assume a role.

"The democratic process of education even affected the relationship of teachers with the administrators. Many school administrators who had once been very autocratic in their relationship with faculty members began to establish standing committees which made recommendations to the administration on professional matters. Teachers in many schools were even encouraged to try out innovative practices and put them to the test of experience.

"Dewey thought that educators should investigate educational methods by putting the methods to the test of experience. He also felt that educators should have a knowledge of the results they are seeking while educating youngsters. Dewey was more concerned with the art of education or practical philosophy of education as opposed to the speculative or theoretical philosophy of education.

"The impact of pragmatism during the 20th Century knew no bounds. Practically every school system in America was directly or indirectly affected. There are literally thousands of schools, particularly in rural areas, which are concerned with providing youngsters with certain moral and spiritual values without teaching religion. Yet, these traditional schools have been affected by the impact of pragmatism."

"Professor, what about denominational schools? Did Pragmatism affect them?"

"Yes, indeed, most definitely. Now you must remember this one point whether you find it acceptable or unacceptable. Practically every denominational school, whether a Catholic, Baptist, Presbyterian, Methodist or any other major denominational church school in America, will fight to the death on one point, namely, speculative philosophy has a bearing on practical philosophy. Parents send their youngsters to denominational schools and colleges because they want their youngsters to study or be exposed to certain religious values. However, the impact of pragmatism can be found in practically all denominational schools.

"One can observe the influence of pragmatism by looking at the curriculum, instructional aids and materials, particularly in the sciences and social studies. Pragmatism could be likened to a virus in that it had no regard for race, color or creed. Pragmatism opened the windows and was a fresh new breeze. It radically changed the 'Art of Education' in America.

"Because of the impact of pragmatism, there are those who believe that the denominational schools in America are the best denominational schools in the world. They also add that public schools in America are the finest public schools in the world because of the impact of both traditionalism and pragmatism.

"At any rate, the wave of pragmatism had come in and nothing could roll back the tide. Once tasted, it seemed unlikely that either American teachers or youngsters would ever give up their small taste of freedom. They liked the idea of the democratic process and it seemed that that process was here to stay. The existentialist, however, had not, as yet, been reckoned with and he was anxious to have his day in court.

"So, tomorrow, the existentialist."

Reality is Existing

Chapter Nine

EXISTENTIALISM

"Today we are going to talk about existentialism, our fifth and last philosophical camp. Existentialism may be traced back to the first half of the 19th Century, to Soren Kierkegaard, a Danish philosopher who was primarily concerned with metaphysical questions. Kierkegaard's works were not translated into English until the 20th Century.

"Shortly after World War II, just when many traditionalists were beginning to accept much of the practical philosophy of the pragmatists, the existentialists began to fan the fires of educational thought. Some educators think that the flames from the fire are scorching a great many of American schools, while others believe that the glow from the fire represents a beacon of hope. However, that will be a question for each of you to decide.

"The existentialists could not accept the traditionalist's view that an essential body of knowledge must be imparted to all youngsters, nor the idea that speculative philosophy gives man the right kind of convictions which will enable him to achieve his final destiny.

"Pragmatism was unacceptable to the existentialists because everything seemed to revolve around the idea of social acceptability. That is, if society agreed, then it was per-

89

missible. They also felt the pragmatists overemphasized the scientific method and ignored the emotional aspects of man.

"The existentialists advocated an educational philosophy which was predicated on the idea that each individual should be the ultimate chooser in all things. It is the individual, not speculative philosophy, nor society, who should determine man's destiny.

"The existentialist, rather than accept the ontology of mind, things, being or experience, simply states that reality is a world of man's existence. He states, I exist, therefore, I am. No one can deny man's existence and, because he exists, he has the power to control his own destiny by making decisions or choices which are good for him. The existentialist believes that man is emerging and becoming and may attain his human potential by making choices. He believes that man, and only man, has the responsibility for making these choices. In other words, the existentialist believes that existence precedes essence and man will achieve his essence after his existence."

"Professor."

"Yes, ma'am."

"Well, when I hear that existence precedes essence or that essence precedes existence, very frankly, I just don't understand what the problem is really about. Can you explain what is meant by, uh, well, particularly, the word essence?"

"Well, I'll try. If we can clarify the meaning of essence, then maybe it will be simple for everyone. The word essence can be used in talking about an odor, or perfume. We may refer to its essence. We may use the word essence in talking about the most significant property of a thing. When one says the essence of the matter is . . . he may really be saying something to the effect that the heart of the matter is . . . or, the real nature of the problem is . . . or, the crux of the matter is . . . or some other similar expression.

"However, the word essence, as it is used here, really refers to the ultimate nature of man. This is a very important factor in the ontological argument. The Thomists, along with the overwhelming majority of all religious demoninations, believe that essence precedes existence. When they say that essence precedes existence, they mean that the nature of man's existence, his very essence, the idea of man, existed in the mind of God. For example, the Thomists believe that, after God created man, He decided it was not good for man to live alone. So, after creating Adam in His own image, He took a rib from Adam and created Eve from His idea of woman. The Thomists believe that the notion or idea of man's creation is the essence of man's existence. Man was created because it was good.

"The existentialists believe that man exists first. Sort of like saying, here I am and I may behold the wonders of the universe. It is the individual who emerges and struggles to achieve his essence. Man achieves essence by making discoveries about himself and understanding that he is a unique person who can control his destiny by making his own choices. In order to become a fully functioning individual, man must accept total responsibility for his choices. It is the right and the responsibility of every individual to choose for himself. Each individual must choose, or choose not to choose. The existentialist is very emphatic on one point. It is the individual, not society nor speculative truths, which will decide the course of action which he will follow. Every individual must decide for himself; every individual is completely free to be the ultimate chooser in all things and must accept the burden of the consequences of his choices. Ultimately, if man chooses wisely, he may fulfill his potential and achieve his essence."

"Professor, if the existentialists reject the notion that essence precedes existence, then does this mean that an existentialist must then be an atheist or one who rebels against society?"

"Well, now, I think in all fairness I would be doing an existentialist an injustice if I were to imply that he was some sort of a nut who is in continual conflict with society and God. Although the expression 'Existence precedes Essence' may be considered as atheistic, an existentialist may be theistic. An existentialist may simply choose to believe in the possibility of God's existence. In the final analysis, he will say that he thought the matter through and he chose to believe that it may be possible for God to exist. Existential Theology is not based on the acceptance of God's word or authority. It is pure choice. As far as society is concerned, an existentialist may agree with society, say, regarding a law which society has passed. But he will not necessarily agree with the law just because society has passed it. He agrees because he chooses to agree."

"Well, now, professor, practically everyone has had some disagreement with certain laws and yet they obey the law. Do you mean that an existentialist would not obey any law with which he disagreed?"

"No, not exactly; he may or he may not. Let's use this example. We will assume that I am an existentialist who drives a car every day on a very lonely road and the county authorities put a stop light in the middle of the road. Now, every time I approach the light, I just drive on through because there is no one around and I feel that the light doesn't belong there anyway since there is no intersecting road. Then, one day, as I am driving, I see a police car parked nearby. Then I may, if I wish, pull up and stop and obey the traffic light."

"But, professor, how can you do that if you say you are an existentialist? If you believe that the light shouldn't be there, how can you compromise your principles by stopping?"

"Your question is exactly the point I want to make and this is where the existentialist will fight to the death. The existentialist will say that, although he believes the light should not be there, he may choose to stop. Now, one may argue that I really chose to stop because of the police car, an instrument of society, which was parked nearby, and society told me to stop. Now, if I were a true existentialist, I would simply state that I chose to stop and neither society nor the police car made me stop. Stopping was my decision, and mine alone. I chose to stop rather than suffer the consequences. Man may choose to obey, choose not to obey, or choose not to choose.

"The final decision of choice is still left up to the individual and, regardless of what 'speculative philosophy' or 'society' says, the individual must be, and is, the ultimate chooser. However, there is a burden of responsibility connected with man's choices and man must assume the responsibility of his actions. The existentialist believes that it is man who chooses. Even if man is coerced to agree with society or speculative philosophy through the use of fear, the final choice is still man's.

"Now, let me repeat that it would be erroneous for me to infer that the existentialists are anti-society or anti-tradition because an existentialist may, if he wishes, choose to agree with society or tradition. There are an extremely large number of existentialists who are good, upstanding, responsible citizens, who are making a very fine contribution to society. However, there are those who believe that, if a person were in continuous conflict with society and speculative philosophy, he probably may feel more at home with existentialism, particularly if his life style were somewhat unusual."

"Professor, what about the concept of goodness and beauty?"

"Well, the traditionalist talked about the good being inherent in the object and beauty being related to the pursuit of the Absolute. The pragmatist said that things were neither good nor bad in themselves apart from their effects, and beauty was determined by the public taste—social acceptability. The existentialist believes that the good and the beautiful are pure unadulterated choices of the individual. Goodness and beauty will reside in the mind or the eye of the beholder. Therefore, it is argued that the learner in school is not a microcosmic mind of the idealist, the sense mechanism of the realist, the rational and spiritual being of the Thomist, or the experiencing organism of the pragmatist. The learner is now and always will be the ultimate chooser."

"Professor, do you mean that the learner, not the teacher, nor society, will and should make the ultimate decisions in school?"

"Well, now, there are many shades of gray and I suppose there are still situations where even some existentialists may disagree. Let me first point out how existentialism affected public education and you may decide the answer for yourself.

"Probably one of the major contributions in education has come from the area of guidance and counseling. Now guidance is when a youngster may ask you to help him make out a schedule and you provide the necessary information in order to guide him in accordance with his capabilities. Counseling is different in that you may counsel a student about a personal problem which may or may not be related to school.

"One method of counseling students is referred to as the autocratic approach or the directive method, which the existentialists charge that all traditionalists use. If a youngster went to a counselor who was a traditionalist and said that he was thinking about quitting school and wanted the counselor's advice, the counselor would definitely tell him. The end result, regardless of the youngster's reasons, would be that the counselor, in all probability, would point out many reasons why the youngster should stay in school. The counselor would probably be very directive and explain to the youngster why it would be a mistake to quit school.

"The existentialists believe that the directive method or the autocratic approach in counseling is entirely wrong. Man exists—he is becoming, and since he is the ultimate chooser, youngsters must be taught to make their own choices and accept the responsibility for their decisions. The existentialists believe in the nondirective method of counseling or the client-centered approach. The main thing to remember is that one should not tell any youngster what he ought to do when he is being counseled. The youngster must be encouraged to make decisions for himself."

"Well, professor, to me, that really seems like it's just a good way for the counselor to wash his hands of the problems so he won't be bothered with a student's personal problem."

"No, no, I didn't mean to infer that at all. Let's take the youngster who says he is thinking about quitting school. Now, the existentialists believe that we are just kidding ourselves if we lecture the youngsters and point out why they should stay in school. They say that if we want to modify a pupil's behavior, we must first enable him to understand the problem and how he relates to the total problem, as well as the consequences of any decision he might make. If a student is wrong, he must first understand he is wrong, next admit he is wrong, and then accept the consequences.

"Now, the counselor, who is an existentialist, believes that he must first establish rapport with the client. The client must feel free to say anything without fear of being reproached. The counselor must have empathy, that is, he must be able to put himself in the client's position and really understand how the client feels. The counselor is not going to merely listen for a few minutes and then tell the client that he must decide for himself.

"The counselor will not ask any direct questions, but he may ask how the client 'feels' or how others 'feel'. He may ask how the client's mother 'feels' about his quitting. He may ask if he has thought about where he was going, his future plans, etc., but he would never phrase a question in a threatening way as if he were placing a barrier before the client. The counselor would actually be attempting to subtly raise all the questions or problems which may be related to the problem, such as quitting school. The counselor would, hopefully, try to enable the client to see the total problem with the client right in the center. The counselor sees the client as a hub of a wheel with the spokes being questions for deliberation which may help to lend direction in solving the problem. The counselor never implies by his action or tone of voice that he disapproves of the client. The counselor feels that, for any decision to be valid, it must come from the client. The client must learn how to arrive at decisions and accept the burden of responsibility. The counselor believes that, if an autocratic approach is used and, if it doesn't work, then the client can put the blame on the counselor. The most important reason, however, is that the counselor believes that he has no right to play God and tell the client how he ought to proceed."

"But, professor, don't you think that even if you are using the client-centered approach, you can still lead the client in the direction that 'you' think he ought to go, regardless of how subtle you try to be? Don't you think that the counselor can have an influence on the client's decision by the 'thought provoking' question he raises? Isn't this then still playing God, only in a more subtle manner?"

"Now, that's for you to decide. The existentialist would retort that the counselor could not and should not make the decision."

"Well, suppose the client just felt like he should forget the whole thing and commit suicide?"

"The counselor, who is an existentialist, would still be committed to the client-centered approach and do all he could to enable the client to understand the problem as it is related to him. In the final analysis, it is the client's prerogative to choose his own destiny, even if it's suicide."

"But, professor, I just can't . . ."

"I know, but you will have an opportunity later on to express your point of disagreement. We are not asking that you accept this without question.

"What it all boils down to—the crux of the problem, is that every child should be viewed as the ultimate chooser and it is the responsibility of the teacher to motivate youngsters to fully understand themselves and the curriculum of the school in order that they may learn to choose wisely.

"Of course, we could go to one end of the scale and talk about Summerhill, where youngsters had complete and total freedom at A. S. Neil's boarding school in England. The ideas of Summerhill, although somewhat radical, influenced education in America. Some counterparts of Summerhill sprang up because of federal funding. Somehow the programs were usually modified with built in restraints after the first year of operation.

"When one considers the many new innovative programs which have come into existence since the latter half of the 20th Century, one becomes amazed at the impact of existentialism. Where Dewey's pragmatism had the democratic process of determining what was good, or whether it works in light of the desired results, the existentialists had as the first criterion the choice of the individual.

"The existentialist believes that the primary function of the school is to enable youngsters to really understand themselves, to be able to understand and see themselves as others see them. Then, only then, are they aware of themselves whereby they can accept themselves as others see them. After achieving self-awareness, youngsters are in a better position to understand the meaning and purpose of life. Tradition and society must not be the yardstick for making the final judgment. The judgment must come from the individual.

"The existentialists are largely responsible for taking the child-centered curriculum in a democratic classroom and turning it into an individualized instructional program, a program tailored for each individual. A child may be at the 'traditional' 4th grade level, but may be learning English at the 6th grade level and math at the 3rd grade level. Each youngster would be working at his own rate of speed or capability in each subject. There were and are many different variations of this program whether it is called modular scheduling, non-graded curriculum or open-access curriculum. There are, as you know, many different approaches and names, but they all seem to say something about 'let's take the child from where he is and help him to progress at his own rate of speed as far as he can go,' or words to that effect.

"Phase-elective programs in English and the social studies came into vogue. A school year would be broken up into 4 quarters which means that a youngster in most states needed 16 quarters or 4 years of high school English to graduate. Well, the school could offer around 40 quarters of different English courses at different levels of instruction. An easy 1/4 credit hour course in, say, 'Reading for Enjoyment' would be offered to students who were not planning to attend college as opposed to a 1/4 credit hour course in Shakespeare. Youngsters are able to choose, not only 'phase elective' courses in English, but also social studies, math, science, and choose all their subjects in every area and still meet graduation requirements."

"Professor, how do you prevent a person from doing something, say a good student who has college potential, from choosing all easy courses which meet graduate requirements?"

"That, of course, is a problem, and one which can well happen. One of my colleagues once answered this problem by saying that, if you are an existentialist, you don't 'prevent' a person from doing anything, that would make you, not him, the chooser. However, a vital factor in this type of instructional program would be a good guidance and counseling office in the school. The guidance counselor would be charged with the responsibility of helping and guiding the student in making his own choices. The student's academic record, test results, such as I.Q., achievement, personality, interest, aptitude, psychomotor ability, or any other type of test which he has taken, may be used to help him make decisions. The student's occupational goals will, of course, be the biggest factor, but the final decision will be made by him.

"Once any student or any man becomes aware, truly aware, of his existence in relation to his concept of self, then he will discover that moral choice is inescapable. Whether the choice is to choose, or not to choose, he has reached the Existential Moment, so say the existentialists.

"If pragmatism left an indelible mark on American education, then existentialism may be likened to a branding iron in that it is leaving a fire-brand on every school which it has touched. The brand has not yet healed in many schools, but the brand has been deeply ingrained. Once any individual, whether student or teacher, is allowed complete individual freedom of choice, it is doubtful whether he will be able to settle for anything less in the future.

"Right or wrong, the five philosophies which we have discussed had a definite impact upon education in America. Moreover, it is still too early to assess the ultimate impact of these philosophies. It is especially difficult, at this moment, to measure the impact of existentialism since its influence is still in the indeterminate stage.

"Nevertheless, in order for any philosophy to have validity, it must provide a firm foundation for the development of educational objectives, as well as a rationale which will enable educators to solve practical educational problems.

"It is hoped that, tomorrow, each of you will be able to begin an examination of your own educational philosophy and apply it to practical educational problems.

"If there are no questions or comments, we will adjourn until tomorrow."

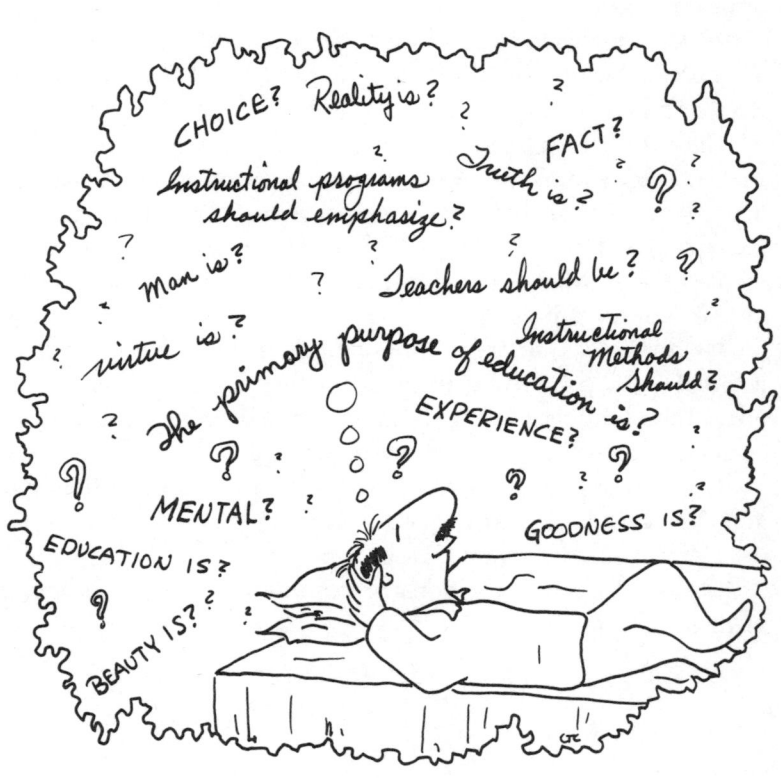

Chapter Ten

THE PROBLEM

"If you will recall, it was pointed out during our first meeting that we were going to concern ourselves with a cursory examination of five different philosophies. It is hoped that we now have a basic understanding as to how metaphysical questions have affected educational practice.

"It was also pointed out that to understand *what* happened without understanding the *why* can have no meaning. In order to understand why, it was necessary that we understand why each philosophical camp subscribes to its particular philosophical position. In all fairness, I should confess that you are probably at a disadvantage in that you have been subjected to my interpretation and I'm sure that there were many metaphysical questions which were never even discussed. Yet, it is impossible to adequately study one particular philosophy in a single seminar, much less five. Regardless of our inadequacies, it is hoped that you do have a basic understanding of the *why*. Each of the five philosophical camps are firm in their beliefs and they are not going to apologize to you or to me. To them, their course of action is clear and they are prepared to do battle.

"We stated during our orientation session that each of us should attempt to formulate his own philosophy of education and understand how his philosophy could be applied to educational practice. To aid you in this endeavor, I have prepared a guide which I would like for you to follow:

A GUIDE FOR WRITING A PHILOSOPHY OF EDUCATION

Instructions: Please choose *one* response in each of the following nine statements whose answers represent (I) Idealism; (R) Realism; (T) Thomism; (P) Pragmatism; and (E) Existentialism. Choose the one response to which you give first priority. Use these statements as an outline and discuss *WHY* you believe your responses should be given first priority in your philosophy of education.

1. Ontology - Reality is: (I) Mental; (R) Matter in Nature; (T) Being; Pure Being or God, logical beings or ideas, and real beings or things; (P) That which man experiences; (E) The fact of man's existence.

2. Epistemology - Truth is: (I) An idea conceptualized by the mind; (R) A fact which is verifiable; (T) Either a practical truth attained through reason or an eternal truth which is self-evident to man because of man's intuition; (P) The result of human experience and the pragmatic test; (E) The choice of the individual.

3. Axiology; Ethics - Goodness is: (I) The emulation of the Macrocosmic or Absolute Mind; (R) Man's conformity to the nature of the universe; (T) A reasonable action resulting from rational thought; (P) That which meets socially acceptable standards; (E) The choice of each individual.

4. Axiology; Aesthetics - Beauty is: (I) The ideal or utopian image; (R) A realistic or natural image; (T) That which is pleasing to the intellect; (P) That which is pleasing to society; (E) The choice of each individual.

5. The primary purpose of education is to: (I) Transmit ideas, ideals and the cultural heritage; (R) Transmit factual knowledge; (T) Develop the intellect and instill moral and spiritual values; (P) Provide experiences in problem solving; (E) Provide education for choice.

6. Man is perceived as a student: (I) With a microcosmic mind; (R) Who responds to the stimuli in nature; (T) Composed of body and soul which are inseparable until death; (P) Who learns through experience; (E) Who is the ultimate chooser.

7. The Instructional program should emphasize: (I) The communicative arts and ideas; (R) The physical and natural sciences; (T) Mental and spiritual development; (P) The student experiencing social problems; (E) Each individual making his own choice.

8. The educative process should utilize methods primarily concerned with: (I) Instilling ideas and ideals by using lectures and class discussions; (R) Teaching facts needed for the physical world by using lectures, demonstrations, and recitation; (T) Developing the mind and the spirit by using lecture, drill and catechism; (P) Finding solutions to social problems; (E) Elaborating awareness of choice.

9. The teacher is perceived as one who: (I) Is a paragon of virtue; (R) Performs demonstrations; (T) Ministers the mind and the soul; (P) Is a democratic coordinator of the problem solving process; (E) Facilitates the individuals choosing process.

"After you have indicated your choice regarding each statement on this guide, you are to write and tell why you believe what you have chosen. The important thing is that you do choose and understand *why*. It is quite possible that many of you may wish to pick several responses for each statement. For example, I'm sure that there are people here who believe that the method of educating or the instructional program may or should be concerned with more than one single answer. We aren't asking you to deny the importance of the other choices in each statement. You are to choose the one single response in which you place the highest value.

"As far as I'm concerned, my role is not to judge who is wrong or who is right. We can always engage in semantics and give our own interpretation to terminology and in the final analysis still be pretty much in agreement, particularly on the practical questions of how we ought to educate."

"Professor, if we choose an ontology, say, the ontology of mind, for example, then does this mean that our epistemology should be an idea and then go straight down the line through the philosophical beliefs of the idealists? I'm not sure that I can wholeheartedly agree with any one philosophical camp."

"Well, I can understand that and you certainly are not alone in your view. There are those who believe that one does not have a true philosophy of education unless all nine responses are from the same philosophical camp. For example, if you choose to believe that reality is mental, then truth would be an idea; your values would be an emulation of the ideal. Therefore, the purpose of education would be to transmit ideas and ideals and the student would be viewed as a microcosmic mind. The instructional program would emphasize the communication arts, and the educational process would utilize methods primarily concerned with instilling ideas and ideals by using lectures and class discussions. The teacher would be perceived as a paragon of virtue. Whether you agree or not, many people say your philosophy is not valid unless it is internally harmonious and consistent.

"Yet there are many people, and their number seems to be increasing with every generation, who feel that it is impossible for them, in all good conscience, to go straight down the line. It may be helpful to keep in mind the *differences* between speculative philosophy and practical philosophy. There are those who believe that speculative philosophy is supposed to give man the right kind of convictions which would enable him to pursue his final destiny while practical philosophy would tell him how to proceed. There are others who do not accept the idea that speculative philosophy has a bearing on practical philosophy. Also, many believe in Absolute Truths and yet maintain that the method of educating should enable youngsters to achieve self-awareness.

"Let me share the word *eclectic* with you. An *eclectic philosophy* would be one which would consist of the philosophical beliefs of *two or more* camps. It is not unusual for a great many people to choose, say their speculative philosophy, from tradition, and their practical philosophy from pragmatism and/or existentialism.

"Another example of using the term eclectic could be related to counseling. We talked about the *directive* or *autocratic* method and the *nondirective* or *client-centered* method of counseling. Although we pointed out that the traditionalist may be directive and the existentialist nondirective, one may be *eclectic*. An eclectic approach means that sometimes you would be directive and sometimes nondirective, depending upon the nature of the problem, the age of the individual or many other factors or circumstances.

"In short, what I'm saying is that, if a person wishes, he may choose any camp for each of the nine statements. It is perfectly acceptable to be eclectic. After all, it is your philosophy paper, and the whole point of the paper is to have you wrestle with the problem and really come to grips with *why* do you believe in each of your choices. Are there any questions about your philosophy paper before we proceed?"

"Professor, when are these papers due?"

"They will be due at the conclusion of our seminar. You will not be subject to any more lectures from me. We have used up about one-half of this seminar in which you were a captive audience, listening to what may have been a biased interpretation of five different philosophies. Although I have tried very hard to be objective, always remember that no author or instructor should be taken as gospel. All you ever really receive from a book or an instructor is merely another point of view.

"Another thing, if this seminar is going to make any sense at all, then we need to get out of the realm of the metaphysical and discuss the practical educational problems which are forever emerging in our rapidly changing society. We need to address ourselves to the implications of philosophical thought upon the aims of education, the process of education, the methods or procedures, the instructional program, and the responsibility of teachers, students and society.

"For the remainder of our session today, I want to share some questions with you. Starting tomorrow, we are going to have group discussions in which each of you will be asked to share his convictions on a variety of topics with his group. You must remember our rule, that we all reserve the right to disagree without being disagreeable. When one disagrees, he should, in each case, try and explain why he believes in his position.

"There are those who believe that group discussions may be a waste of time. Those who are unable to listen to an opposing point of view usually claim that we are 'swapping' ignorance. What we must admit, however, is that there are opinions other than our own. When man understands *why* an individual believes the things he believes, then possibly we may become not only more tolerant of one another's views, but we will keep one another from veering to the radical-left or to ultra-conservative right.

"At any rate, here are some problems you may or may not wish to discuss. There are those who believe that the humanities are being neglected and there is a significant body of knowledge which must be transmitted to each generation. Theirs is the great books theory. Certain knowledge has stood the test of time and it is the essentialist who believes that this knowledge must be imparted to youngsters. The pragmatists argue that survival in itself should not determine the validity of subject-matter selection. The pragmatists also maintain that there are many ideas in our society which are false and still persist because they have been handed down.

"The essentialists put much emphasis on utility, as it is believed that knowledge is useful for the sake of knowledge. The pragmatists also acknowledge the principle of utility; however, they charge that there is a lack of social direction. Utility in itself does not indicate the sort of world man would like to build for himself. Utility, say the pragmatists, overlooks the fact of social change. Will what we may be teaching today be useful in later life?

"Another problem is related to the idea of social reconstruction. The *reconstructionists* comprise a branch of pragmatism which believes that schools should reconstruct society. The reconstructionists charge that educators are spending too much time washing yesterday's dishes when they should be planning meals for tomorrow. Schools, according to the reconstructionists, should decide what type of world man wants 30 years from now and educators should devise an educational system which will enable man to live in that world. The big problem is *who* is going to decide what kind of a world man wants—the idealists, realists, thomists, pragmatists, or the existentialists? The reconstructionists say society should decide. That, in itself, is a problem of first magnitude. How can we achieve unity when we have so much diversity?

" There are some realists who believe that America is wasting the academically talented. Our schools spend too much time on the *fads* and *frills* of education such as home economics, driver training, industrial arts and typing. The charge is that there is a difference between *education* and *training.* National standards should be instituted and a national testing system should be utilized at the eighth grade level. They feel that the academically talented should be put in college preparatory schools and given more advanced courses in math and the sciences. Less talented youngsters could go to less demanding high schools for a general diploma or to vocational schools.

"The pragmatists take an opposite view in that they believe that every American public school should have as its primary objective the socialization of the child. Youngsters should mingle with every race, color, or creed during school in order that they may have a better understanding of society. Homogeneous grouping, according to academic ability, is not only undemocratic but also indefensible because a child may feel stigmatized. Then, of course, there are those who go a step further and say that all grading should be abolished and students should receive either an indication of pass or fail. Competition should be abolished and students should be the ultimate choosers in all course requirements.

"The notion that each individual student should be the *ultimate chooser in all things* may seem to represent the radical left, but the problem is there. What about students' rights? Student publications? Expression of ideas? Appearance? Convictions concerning saluting the flag? Academic and personal freedom?

"What about teachers? Should teachers be allowed to join unions and go on strike? Should each teacher be free to decide what he should include in his courses? Should he be free to determine how they shall be taught (free from dictation by community groups or individual citizens)? Should a teacher be able to engage in any activity he chooses outside the academic setting, unless his behavior can be shown to affect his professional teaching performance in an adverse way?

"Should there be censorship in public schools? Should *Othello* be banned because a black king is married to a white queen? Should *Merchant of Venice* be banned because

Shylock is depicted as a greedy Jew? Should *Huckleberry Finn* be banned because a character is called Nigger Jim? Should *Catcher in the Rye* be banned because of some four-letter words? We should keep in mind that the community may be a big factor. For example, the *Merchant of Venice* may be unacceptable in some communities but acceptable in others. At any rate, what is your opinion concerning censorship?

"Most teachers agree that, although they prefer a course title such as Family Living or The Home and the Family, sex education should be taught in schools. This has created a storm of protest in many communities. Some communities have protested and have questioned the validity of teaching sex education or the use of various instructional aids. Many people believe that the school should include the teaching of the morality of sex. If so, whose morals do you teach?

"There are those who have expressed concern about the teacher's role and the teacher's responsibility. Should moral and spiritual values be instilled in youngsters? If not, why not? If so, whose values are you going to impart? Tradition's? Society's? Your own? Or are you going to tell the youngster to decide for himself? Suppose a young junior or senior high school girl asks if she should become intimate with her boyfriend, start taking the pill, or get an abortion? What then is the role of the teacher or the counselor in this case? Suppose this was your daughter. The problem here is that even parents cannot decide easily what course of action to take. Yet, they expect the school to be able to resolve their problems for them.

"The problem of discipline is reputed by many to be of very serious magnitude. Thousands of teachers have been assaulted by students. Policemen are on hall duty in many large schools. What about discipline? How should we discipline youngsters? What constitutes a juvenile delinquent and what is the school's responsibility to a delinquent student? Is it the responsibility of schools to instill socially acceptable habits of conduct? Who determines such conduct? Are students free to choose their own acceptable standards of behavior? Who, then, should determine standards? Tradition, society, the teacher, or each individual student?

"You know, we could go on and on raising questions and I'm sure there may be other questions or problems in which you are more interested. I am going to ask each of you to write out two questions or topics which you would like to discuss. We will divide up into small groups. But, before you begin discussion on your individual questions, I would like for each group first to discuss and then write out the purposes or the objectives of education in America. Just what should education do? What should we expect our schools to accomplish? I would like for you to keep in mind that it is impossible for schools to teach everything and it is impossible for youngsters to learn everything. Therefore, what should be taught and what should be expected of youngsters to learn? These questions are just merely points to keep in mind when you attempt to state the purpose of education in America.

"Should the educational philosophy in America be rooted in only one philosophical camp? If so, where? Tradition? Pragmatism? Or Existentialism? Is Eclecticism an obscenity? Is it possible, in a nation with so much diversity to achieve a unity of purpose in education? Can an eclectic philosophy provide an educational objective with a concern for values, and essential knowledge, a concern for producing youngsters who are able to function in a free society, and a concern for producing a youngster who has been motivated in achieving self-awareness.

"The problem is interesting. Society will continue to change and we must always re-evaluate our educational objectives. This is what makes philosophy interesting. If we neglect to re-define our objectives, then we will always continue to teach the same old things in the same old way.

"Tomorrow, thank Heavens, I'm going to shut up and sit down. You people will really get an opportunity to get involved. You are no different than all other teachers. I know you have opinions and, if teachers are not qualified to lend direction to the educational enterprise, then I don't know who is.

"I have done all the damage I can do. I think we are ready to really have a very interesting seminar. If so, it will be due to your input in our group discussions.

"Are there any questions? All right. I'll see you tomorrow."

The professor paused and watched the teachers leave the seminar. He really felt pleased. He felt that he had been able to establish a good rapport with the participants, particularly after the first couple of days. By and large, most of the teachers seemed to be genuinely interested in the seminar, thus far, even though he had spent a lot of time lecturing.

The professor felt that the ground work was laid and the rest of the seminar was finally going to be a seminar in the true sense of the word. He walked away with the feeling that the proposed group discussions were going to be very interesting to observe. Somehow, he just knew it. He really felt good, so good that he could hardly wait to see what would transpire.

"I have no other alternative but to choose between what *I am* and what I can *become*."

Chapter Eleven

THE EXISTENTIAL MOMENT

The pilot's voice broke the silence as the whisper jet was soaring through the stratosphere. "Please fasten your seat belts. Flight 577 to Chicago will be landing at O'Hare Airport in ten minutes. Kindly remain seated until the plane comes to a complete stop. It was a pleasure to have you with us and thank you for flying American."
As the stewardess went down the aisle, she stopped and gently touched the professor. "Please fasten your seat belt, sir. Flight 577 is arriving at Chicago."
The professor seemed startled. "What? Education 577 is landing at Chicago?" He looked out the window and saw the clouds, but there were no people on them. Suddenly he realized that he had been dreaming. In order to be sure, he looked out the window and scanned the sky and the earth. He eagerly looked all around the inside of the plane for assurance. Yes, he had been dreaming. He seemed embarrassed, but he turned to the stewardess, smiled and said, "Thank you, young lady." The professor fastened his seat belt and began to think about his dream. He couldn't believe it. Somehow it had all seemed so real. He recalled the flashbacks on that television thing they called a visualographer. He remembered those episodes which depicted him teaching in high school and at the

university. That was real; those things actually happened. The professor knew he could not escape the implications of his dream.

Oh, yes. What was that eerie feeling he felt after his experience with the visualographer? He remembered he felt a spiritual kinship with Scrooge and the ghost of Christmas past. Pete had said, "You have become an arrogant, self-centered, egotistical, self-serving individual who spends his time trying to impress others with his brilliance."

The professor remembered the remorse he felt during the dream. Could this be true? Where did truth lie? One could always rationalize and offer biased reasons for his actions. The dream had, however, caused him to go through a process of self-evaluation. Isn't that why he had thought that he would gladly teach at that "other receiving station" if he could only walk into a class again and actually establish some rapport with students?

The professor was preoccupied with the dream from the time he awoke until he finally checked into his room at the Conrad Hilton. He had originally planned to freshen up, go out to dinner, then retire in order to be refreshed and at his best in the morning. He had so much wanted to make a good impression with his paper. What did Pete say about an individual who spends his time trying to impress others with his brilliance? Yes, that was it. Yes, he had so much wanted to impress others because he felt that was the key to rising in the university world. He knew that Pete was right when he reminded him that "philosophy does not bake any bread." The more the professor thought about the seminar on Cloud Nine, the more he regretted waking up before the seminar was over. The more he thought about the seminar, the more he wondered how the last half of the seminar turned out.

The professor began to wonder about his philosophy course. Although speculative philosophy is important, was he spending too much time in the realm of the metaphysical? Even the paper he had prepared for presentation to the society was full of metaphysical jargon. Did his paper really make any difference? Was it that important? Would it bake any bread?

The professor wondered if a seminar such as the one on Cloud Nine could be very effective in his philosophy of education class. It seemed to make sense, particularly the part where students could get involved and come to grips with real live educational problems. The professor, after much soul searching, finally realized that, as far as his professional future was concerned, he had reached his *existential moment*.

The professor's moment of truth arrived and he eagerly made his decision. He decided to write another speech for presentation to the society. He was going to point out the real, true purpose of a philosophy of education course. What should it do for students? The professor began to write and the words seemed to flow like magic. He recalled the philosophical objectives he had given to the seminar. The objectives seemed imprinted in his brain. We should have a basic understanding as to how metaphysical questions affected educational practice. To understand *what* happened without the *why* can have no meaning. Students should attempt to formulate their own philosophy and understand how their philosophy could be applied to educational practice. The professor wrote on into the night . . .

At last, he was finished. The professor re-read his new speech, made a few corrections, and felt that he had undergone complete metamorphosis. Strangely, although it was late, the professor was not tired. He was perfectly relaxed and was eagerly waiting to present his newly prepared paper, not because he was trying to impress the Society, but because he had something important to say. The professor left a call to be awakened at seven and then retired for the night.

The next morning, the professor awoke in great spirits. Although he had only about three hours sleep, he felt wonderful. He had a good breakfast and then went to the main ballroom for the general assembly of the members of the Society. After greeting many of his colleagues and acquaintances, the professor put his newly prepared speech inside his breast pocket and took his seat on the platform.

The huge ballroom was almost filled to capacity and many latecomers were quickly scurrying to find vacant seats. The professor self-consciously gazed over the large gathering and began to sort out the many familiar faces. There was old Cornelius Wolfgang who had served as the major professor on Brainhare's doctoral committee. Wolfgang's hair was still flaming red and Brainhare wondered if it had been dyed.

In the row behind Wolfgang sat Cyrus Dennison, a distinguished professor of education from State University, who once was considered to be one of the brightest stars among pedagogical philosophers. Dennison's star had plummeted since he allied himself with a group of radicals who had denounced metaphysics and proclaimed that they were going to concern themselves primarily with questions related to accountability in public education.

As the professor began to reflect upon his Cloud Nine experience, he could easily understand why Dennison had taken such a strong position concerning accountability in public education. His thoughts turned to many questions which were related to his newly prepared speech. Should public schools be held accountable for the products they are producing? Are competency based teacher education programs of any significance? Should schools be expected to outline specific behavioral objectives related to both the cognitive and affective domain in learning? What is the role or purpose of public education? If students cannot learn everything and if schools cannot teach everything, what should schools teach and what should students be expected to learn?

Finally, the program chairman began his introduction of the professor by saying, "And now, ladies and gentlemen, it is a distinct honor and pleasure to present our next reader. This is a gentleman, whom you all know, one who is admired and respected by philosophers everywhere. An erudite colleague who has a unique talent for taking metaphysical principles and synthesizing them into a meaningful context and relating them to the whole epistemological process. His concern for the metaphysical nature of education is evident in his writings, which are valued by scholars everywhere. Ladies and gentlemen, your next reader, Dr. A. Dudley Brainhare."

The professor seemed startled at the mention of his name, and he quickly glanced at the vast audience as the applause filled the ballroom. He could see Wolfgang applauding vigorously with his red hair tossing wildly as he nodded his approval. Brainhare was one of Wolfgang's prized pupils, and it was Wolfgang who had awakened Brainhare's interest in metaphysical principles.

As the professor looked around the ballroom, his mind quickly reflected upon his many trials and tribulations as an academician in higher education. It seemed that it was only yesterday that he was an assistant professor struggling for recognition and hoping that, somehow, he would someday be promoted to associate. Now, here he was, a full professor of education, receiving a very rousing reception from his peers.

In that fleeting instant, the professor seemed overcome by his introduction. This was the moment for which he had been waiting. He never dreamed that he would finally achieve the status he had been seeking for so long. If only the dean of his college and the president of his university could have heard his introduction.

The professor rose and approached the podium. He reached into his breast pocket and fingered his newly prepared speech. Never had he felt such exhilaration. The applause was more than he could bear. He paused momentarily, removed an empty hand from inside his coat and then reached into his hip pocket. He removed and unfolded a number of papers and looked over the large assembly. When the applause died down, he assumed what he believed to be his most scholarly countenance, and in his very best professorial tone, began to read:

A Metaphysical Investigation of the Ontological and Epistemological Processes Involved in the Development of a Logic to Support the Theory of Parallelism

Metaphysically speaking, if one were to examine the epistemological processes involved in the investigation of the theory of parallelism, one must begin with Ontology. Ontologically, if one considers any single being, any matter, whether we call it a macrocosm or God, its being will unfold and its reality will be manifested in two forms: (1) The form of a corporeal world (sub attributo extensionis) and (2) In the form of a world of consciousness (sub attributo cogitationis.) There is a regular relationship without any specific interaction between the psychical and the physical worlds. A parallelism occurs in both, which implies that whatever occurs in the corporeal world as movement (modus extentionis) appears in the world of mind as ideas (idea modus cogitationis.)

Two basic premises are involved in the theory of parallelism: (1) Psychical phenomena are not the end products of physical processes; and (2) Physical phenomena are not the end products of physical processes. Spinoza attempted to substitute an epistemological parallelism for metaphysical parallelism. Many believe that Spinoza employed the parallelism of the psychical and physical world and arrived at an unsatisfactory solution to the metaphysical question: What is the relationship between thought and being? Spinoza believed . . .

Sometimes we end up in a box . . . . not of our own making . . . . .